AF574415

OLD WORLD LACE

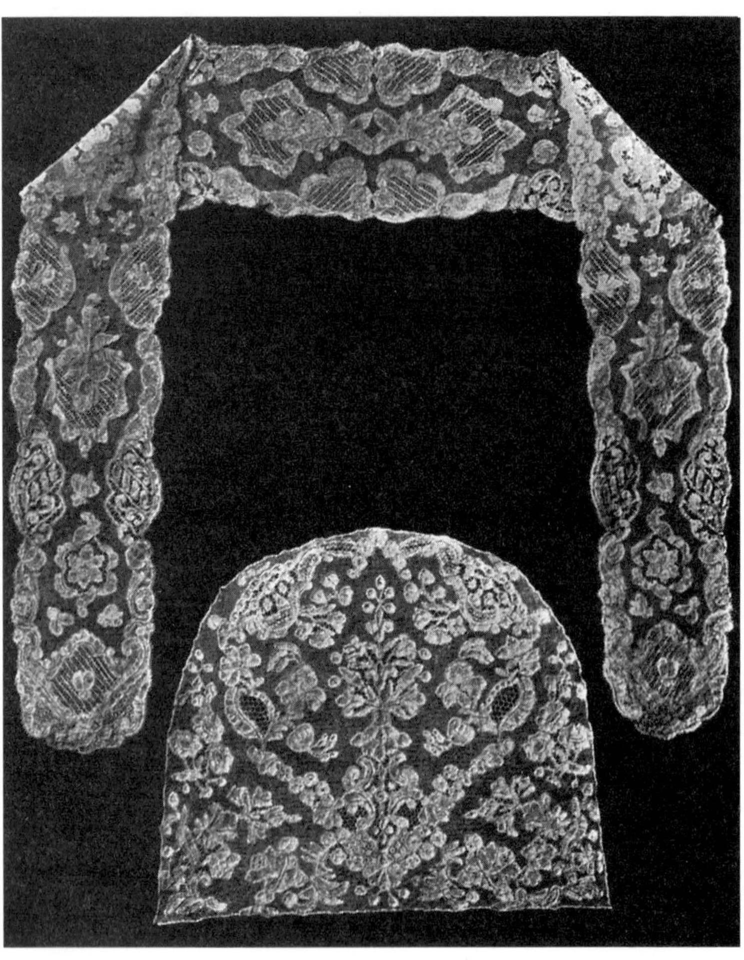

OLD WORLD LACE

A Concise Illustrated Guide

Clara M. Blum

DOVER PUBLICATIONS, INC.
Mineola, New York

"To cultivate the sense of the beautiful is but one, and the most effectual, of the ways of cultivating an appreciation of the Divine goodness."—BOVEE

Published in Canada by General Publishing Company, Ltd., 895 Don Mills Road, 400–2 Park Centre, Toronto, Ontario M3C 1W3.

Published in the United Kingdom by David & Charles, Brunel House, Forde Close, Newton Abbot, Devon TQ12 4PU.

Bibliographical Note

Old World Lace: A Concise Illustrated Guide, first published in 2002, is an unabridged republication of the work originally published in 1920 by E. P. Dutton & Co., New York under the title *Old World Lace or A Guide for the Lace Lover.*

Library of Congress Cataloging-in-Publication Data

Blum, Clara M.
Old world lace : a concise illustrated guide / Clara M. Blum.
p. cm.
"An unabridged republication of the work originally published in 1920 by E. P. Dutton & Co., New York"—T.p. verso.
Includes index.
ISBN 0-486-42150-3 (pbk.)
1. Lace and lace making—Europe. I. Title.

NK9442 .B57 2002
746.2'2'094—dc21

2002018887

Manufactured in the United States of America
Dover Publications, Inc., 31 East 2nd Street, Mineola, N.Y. 11501

CONTENTS

LIST OF ILLUSTRATIONS

LIST OF ILLUSTRATIONS

Introduction

I have felt, in compiling this booklet, the need of a concise guide for the student of old lace who does not care to go too deeply into the history of lace, or the technicalities of its making, but at the same time wants to familiarize himself with the various types of lace. I cannot help feeling that a wider interest might be awakened, were it possible for one to gain the knowledge, in a simplified form, of the distinguishing characteristics of lace.

There should be a revival of the appreciation of this beautiful art which has remained dormant here in America, due possibly to a certain hesitancy on the part of many in taking up the study of a subject which may seem to them rather formidable, but which in reality may be easily mastered, and take its place in the education of our youth, last but not least in the study of the fine arts.

It is my aim, in this book, to give a general idea, in as few words as possible, and with the aid of numerous illustrations, of the many and varied forms of lace, to what century they belong, and in what country they were made.

Should any one feel, after studying this book, that his interest is sufficiently awakened to warrant a fuller and more detailed knowledge of this fascinating subject, there are any number of excellent works that will take him far into the intricacies of lace-making, too numerous to mention, but that any library can supply.

Although there are many slightly conflicting opinions as to the real beginning of this beautiful work, it is safe to say that what we know today as "lace" came into existence about 1500, or even the latter part of the fifteenth century; but from that time on, the rapid development was quite remarkable, for within a period of about fifty years, lace-making had taken its place in nearly all European countries as an acknowledged industry.

Italy is probably the first country to which we turn for our earliest examples, although many other countries, such as Spain and Flanders, undoubtedly made lace about the same time, and in some few instances even earlier.

The early patterns used in all these countries for any form of linen work, prove to us, however, that in copying the Moorish, Greek and Arabic designs from old bits of fabrics, we may look back to a much earlier civilization, to the real origin of this hand work. What chiefly concerns us here, however, is to follow as briefly as possible the course of lace-making from its established beginning down to modern times.

For this purpose we will take up lace, which in the early sixteenth century was the direct outcome of the elaborate drawn and cut work made in Italy for several centuries previous. The gradual elimination of nearly all the linen ground by the drawing of threads brings us to what was known as Reticello. Once established as an industry, which it soon became, lace was divided into two great classes to which belong all the lace made up to the present time.

These two divisions are known as Point or Needle lace, and Bobbin or Pillow lace. Point lace comprises the laces made with the needle, making use of one stitch in its many and varied forms; that is, the buttonhole stitch. Point lace was made before bobbin lace and to this class belong all the Venetian Points, Alençon. Argentan, Point de France, Brussels Point à l'Aiguille or Point de Gaze, etc.

Bobbin lace, more commonly known as pillow, was made, as the name implies, by the use of bobbins attached to a pillow, the number of these bobbins varying greatly, as many as from ten to many hundreds being used, according to the pattern.

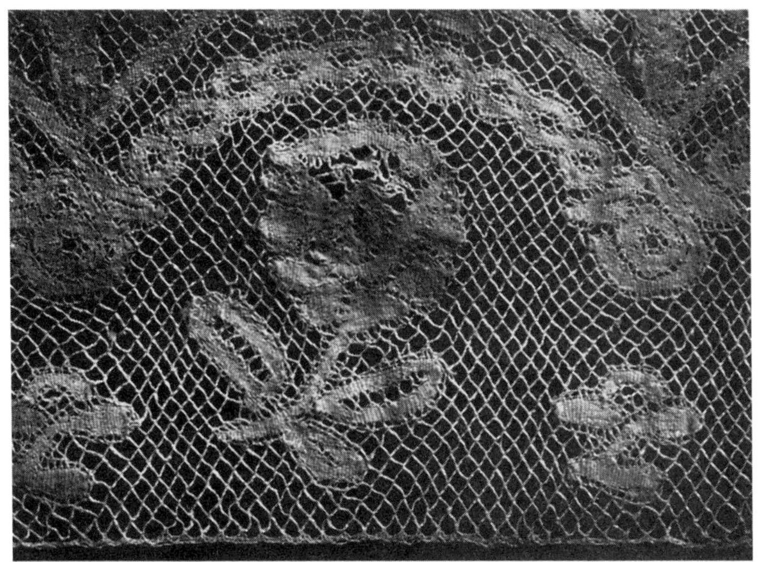

Illustration No. 1
Detail of bobbin toilé

To this class belong Milan, Genoese, nearly all the Spanish laces, Flemish, Point d'Angleterre, Mechlin, Binche, Valenciennes, Point de Paris, Buckinghamshire, Honiton, etc.

Bobbin lace can easily be distinguished from point lace by looking at the execution of the toilé or solid part, which in bobbin lace resembles the crossed and interwoven threads of a woven material, while the solid part of point lace is an easily recognizable needle point stitch.

In the following chapters we will take up the study of the different laces in the order of their development. Italy will be given the first place by right of the undeniable perfection of her early workmanship and the fact that it was in Italy that lace-making first became prominent as an industry. We will try to discuss the lace of each country as clearly as possible, devoting the most detail to the three great lace-making centers of the world, namely, Italy, France and Flanders, and touching

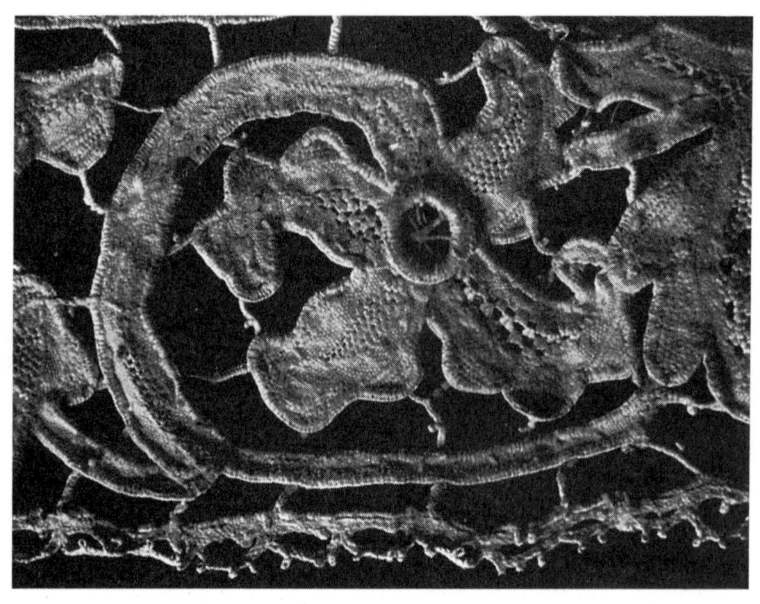

Illustration No. 2
Detail of needle toilé

but lightly on England and Spain. The other European countries all made lace of a certain peasant type which, however, never attained sufficient importance to warrant our devoting space to them in this brief review of laces of greater beauty and value. Any one wishing to go more deeply into the subject of the countless laces of this type, made in all countries, can readily find this information in a comprehensive history of lace, which this book makes no claim to be. The object of this volume is to interest the many whose knowledge of lace lies simply in an appreciation of its beauty, and to give them a simple method of classifying the well-known laces of all countries, thus bringing them to the threshold of a far wider knowledge, and opening for them the portals into the "Kingdom of Lace," where they will be ably guided by Mrs. Palliser, Elisa Ricci, Gertrude Whiting, Mrs. Neville Jackson, and a score of others.

Laces of Italy

Embellishment of personal and household linen as well as vestments of the church, started with what is known as "Punto Tirato" or drawn work, and there is little difficulty in tracing the evolution of this same drawn work into its final phase, known as lace.

The drawing of these threads in greater or less quantities naturally led to the use of a great variety of stitches, among which the satin and curl stitch, or surface embroidery, were used to a great extent, with the "Punto Tagliato" or cut work (where a piece is cut directly out of the material and filled in with a needle stitch), and so on, in various forms, gradually getting further from work on the linen and giving greater attention to the drawn threads.

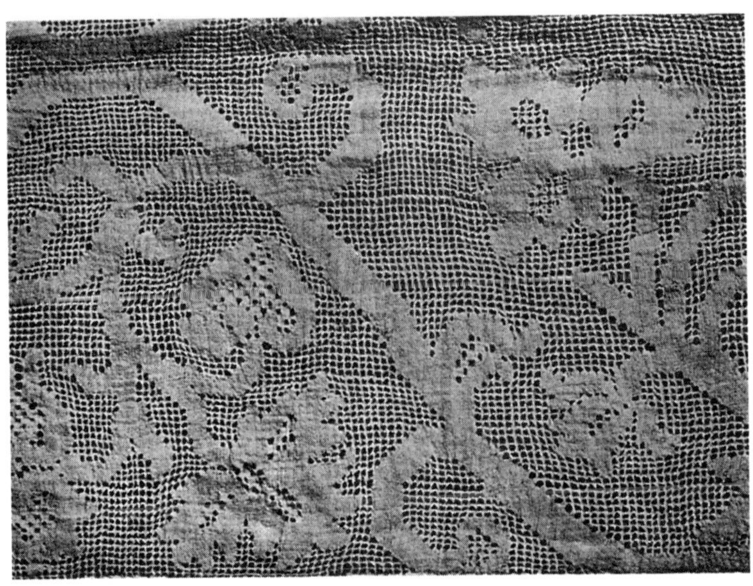

Illustration No. 3
Drawn Linen Work. "Punto Tirato"; 16th century

Illustration No. 4
Cut Work. "Punto Tagliato"; 16th century; showing satin and curl stitch

Reticello

Then comes the next step known as Reticello; this is simply the outcome of the continuous drawing away of

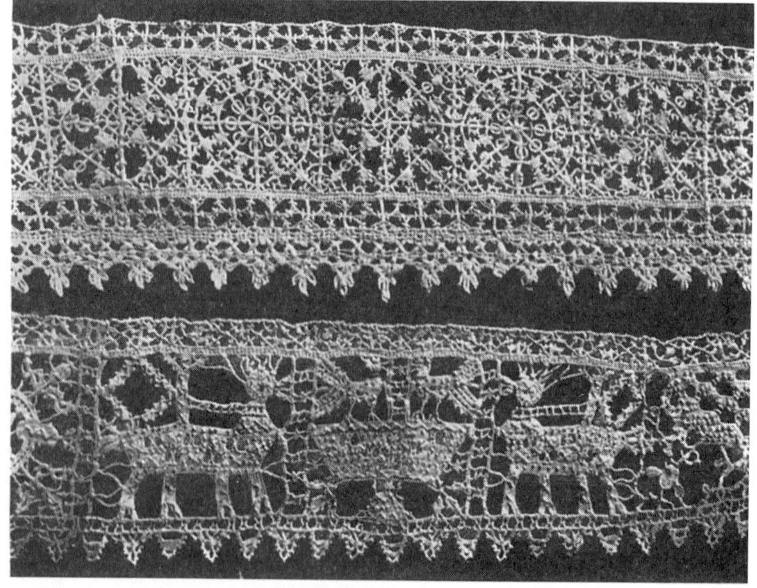

Illustration No. 5
Reticello. Sixteenth century

Illustration No. 6
Reticello Collar. Sixteenth century

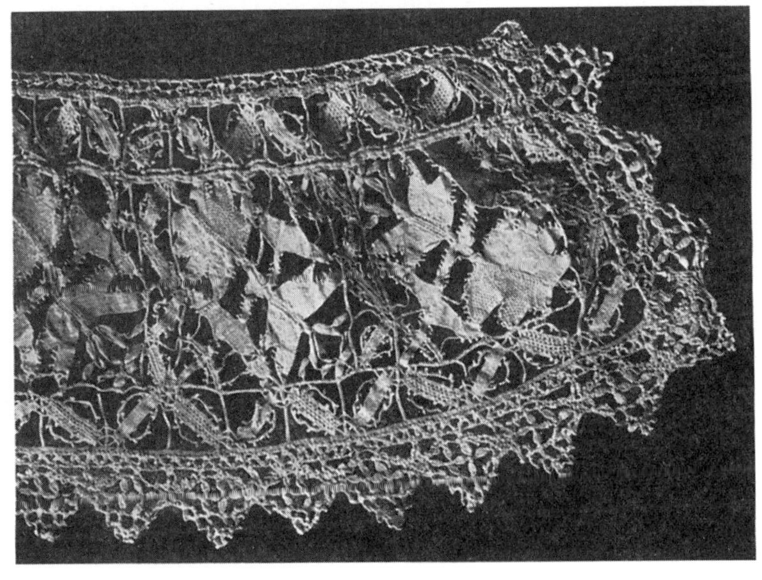

Illustration No. 7
Reticello Collar. Sixteenth century; with bobbin edge

Illustration No. 8

A—Edge of "Punto in Aria." End of 16th century
B—"Punto in Aria." Sixteenth century; showing cardinal tassels in the border

the linen until nothing of it visibly remains. It is the name given to the geometrical borders seen in great quantities of Italian work, which by the few perpendicular lines, to which the connecting link of the linen itself may be easily traced, paved the way in this last great step in linen work for the "Punto in Aria," or the earliest example of what is now known as lace.

Punto in Aria

"Punto in Aria" (stitch in the air), as the name implies, is the final breaking away from any link with the linen material. Its first use was in trimming of various altar cloths, albs, etc., of cut and drawn work. It was made in the form of edges and insertions and closely resembled in stitch and design its forerunner, Reticello. The edge was generally pointed, the sharp being of the earlier period and the shallow, more rounded scallop showing the Spanish influence, belonging to a later date. Some authorities put all Venetian lace under the general head of "Punto in Aria," but I prefer here to call them by their individual names, applying the term "Punto in Aria" only to the earliest stage between Reticello and Gros Point.

From the edges it was but a short and quick step to the lace or beautiful Venetian Points which we know today under the names of Gros Point de Venise, Point Plat de Venise, Coralline, Rosaline and Venise à Réseau.

Gross Point

The first or heavy Venetian Point made with the variation of the buttonhole stitch became richer in design, more complicated in stitch as the workers be-

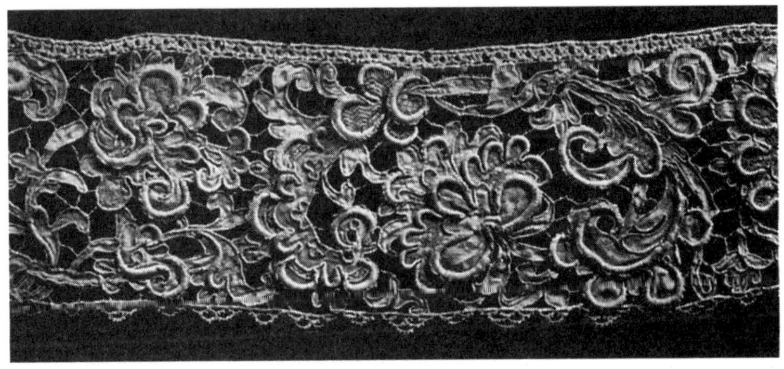

Illustration No. 9
Venetian "Gros Point." Seventeenth century; with brides

Illustration No. 10
Venetian "Gros Point." Detail showing variety of needle stitches

came more efficient. The design, though large, is graceful, and the foliated pattern which is used so much in later Italian lace is seen here for the first time. There

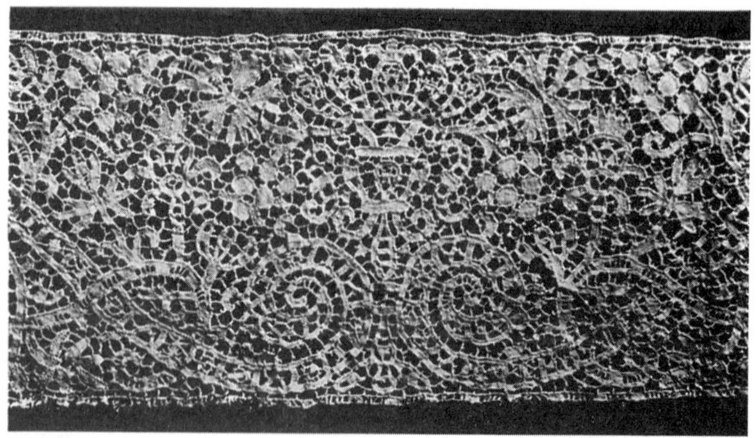

Illustration No. 11
Venetian "Point Plat." Seventeenth century; design with Renaissance scrolls

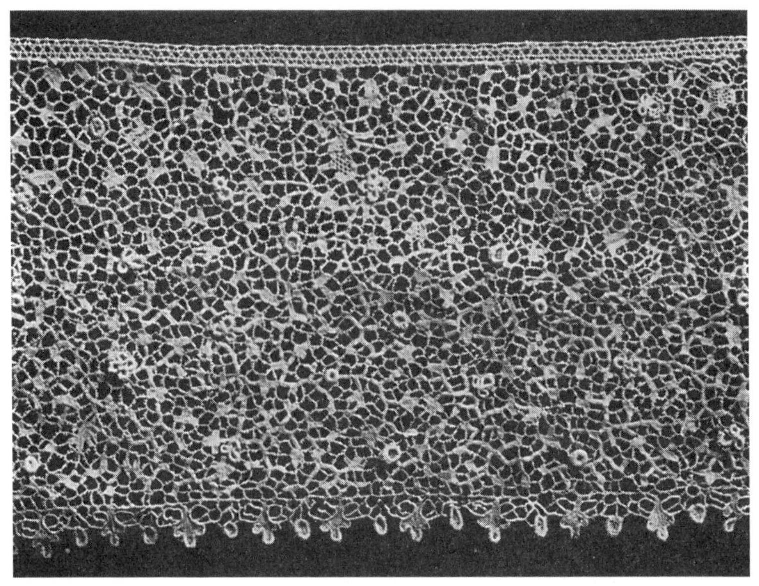

Illustration No. 12
Venetian "Coralline." Seventeenth century

is no background, though in some examples the "motifs" are held together by "brides" or bars made of a fine buttonhole stitch. The heavy cordonnet buttonholed over at various intervals brings out the pattern and is one of the main characteristics of this lace.

The solid parts are made up of a variety of designs, the stitches at times being so close as to give the effect of a linen material, while others are made of open-work designs, checks or other patterns.

Coralline

Following the Gros Point came the flat Venetian or Coralline, very unlike the heavy point in appearance, having its smooth surface unornamented by either the cordon-edged or picotéd flowers. It has no special design save the graceful entwining lines which readily remind one of the coral branches from which it derives its name.

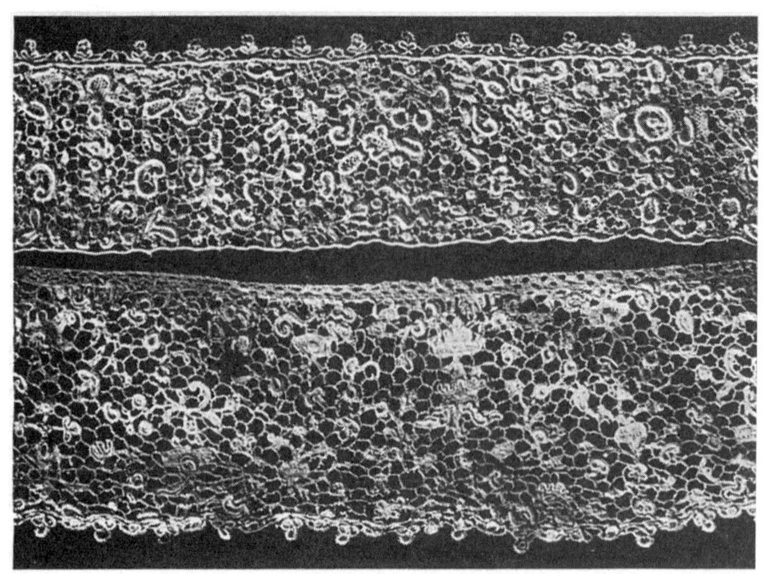

Illustration No. 13
Venetian "Rosaline." Seventeenth century

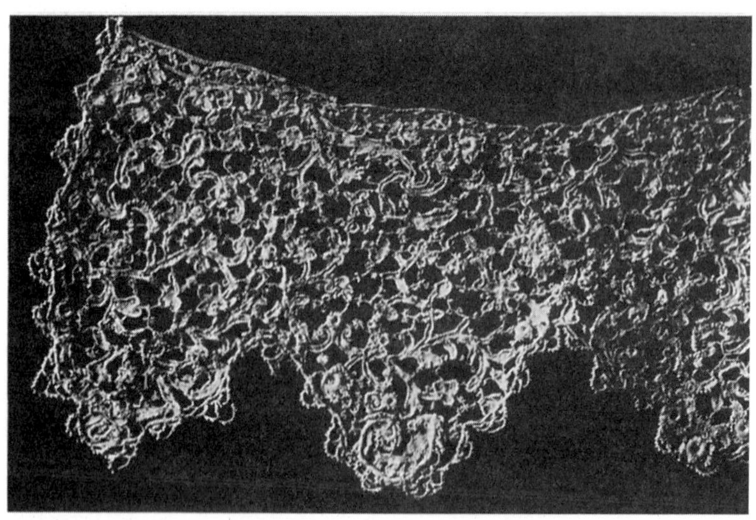

Illustration No. 14
Venetian "Rosaline" Collar. Seventeenth century

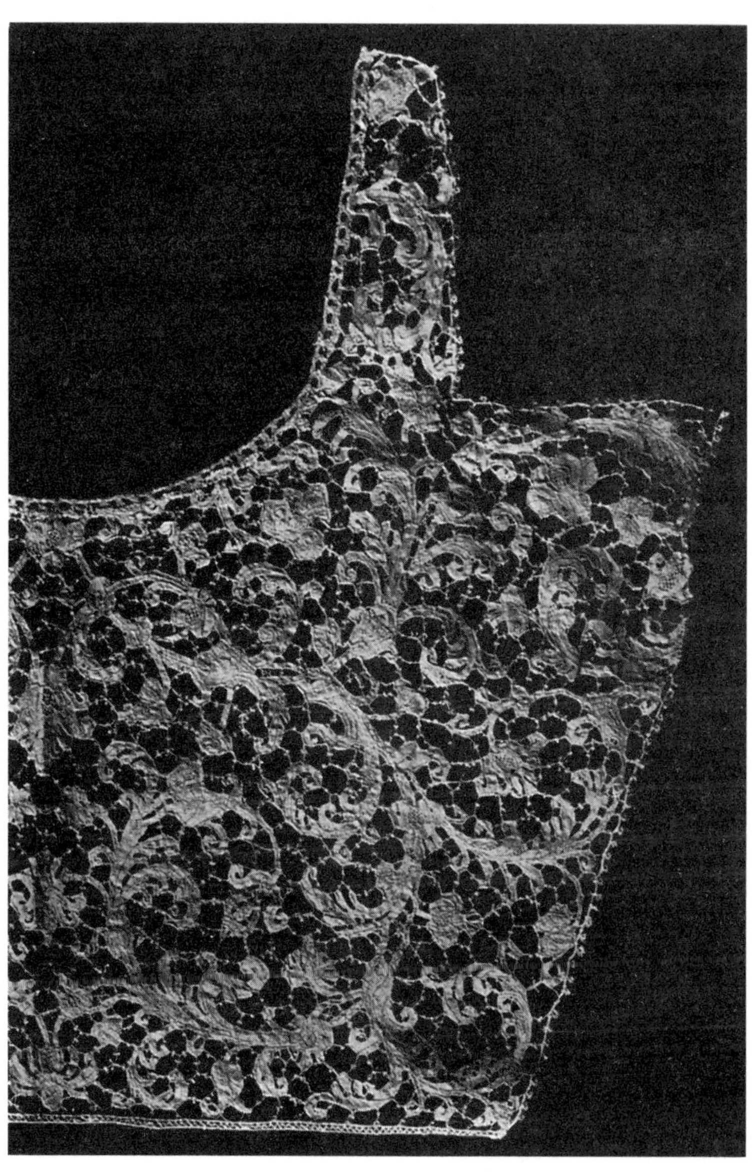

Illustration No. 15
Venetian "Rose Point." Seventeenth century rabat

Rosaline

The Rosaline comes next and its exquisite workmanship makes it among the finest and most sought after of all the Italian laces. It borrows something from both of its predecessors, for while closely resembling the Gros Point in conception, the pattern is much daintier and smaller, making the effect one of airy lightness.

The designs are held together by innumerable tiny "brides" which in turn are profusely ornamented by small rose-like flowers, the edges of the flowers as well as the "brides" are decorated with myriads of little picots, varying of course with the quality of the lace; this gives a raised effect, which is very beautiful.

A type of fine, flat Venise is also called Rose Point, though the rose from which it derives its name is only found ornamenting at intervals the "brides" or bars with a tiny picot-edged circular flower, the main body of the lace resembling the Coralline.

Of course the use of figures, coats-of-arms, or any other designs found in this type of lace adds greatly both to its interest and its value. The distinguishing features, however, remain in the characteristics which we have tried to point out.

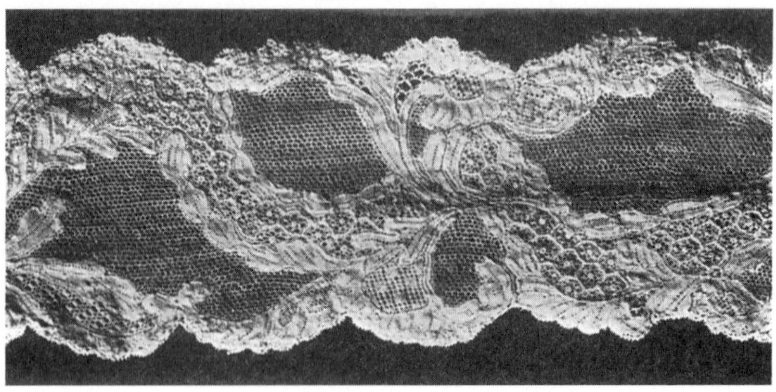

Illustration No. 16

"Venise à Réseau." Eighteenth Century Venetian needle point imitating Alençon

Illustration No. 17
Milan. Bobbin-made without foundation; 17th–18th century

Venise à Réseau

The Venise à Réseau, or grounded Venise, belongs to a considerably later date than the Venetian Points. When Colbert founded the great lace industry in France in 1665, it did not take long for the beautiful Alençon and Argentan laces to find their way into Italy. The beauty of the fine needle-made net or mesh which formed the ground work of these laces, charmed the Italians and they soon set to work to copy this wonderful new ground or Réseau. The result was the combination of the needle point designs, the flower and foliated patterns of the other laces and the fine mesh which the Italian workers soon learned to make. This was called Venise à Réseau. Examples of this exquisite work are rare.

Milan

In describing the Venetian points we have touched on the best known and most sought-after of the needle-made Italian laces, and we now turn to the bobbin-made laces of Milan, which, by their beauty, give ample proof that the women of Milan were as skilled in the use of their bobbins as were their sisters of Venice in plying the needle.

The Milanese lace of the sixteenth and seventeenth centuries, was a flat, tape-like lace, very open as to pattern and generally following little or no design, save the curving circular lines often joined by "brides" and called "flat Milan."

A close examination of this lace will readily show the reader the distinct difference between the toilé or

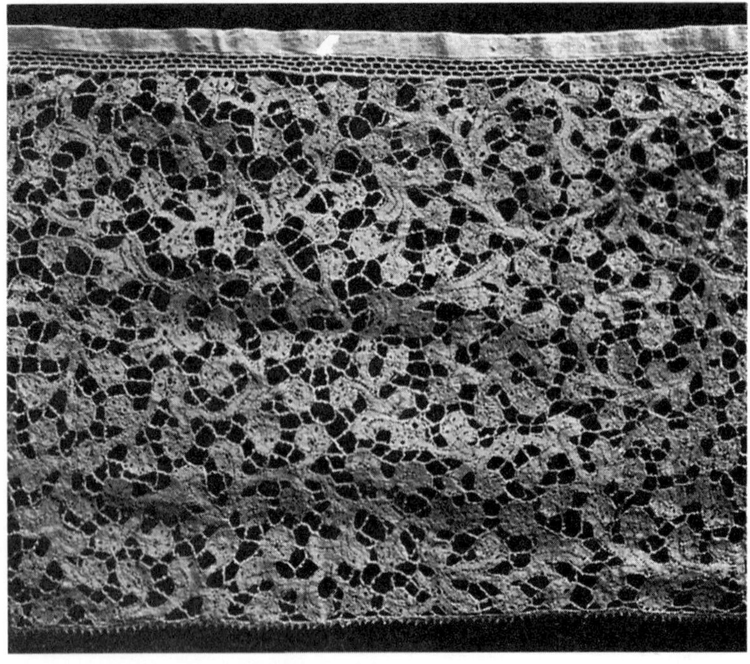

Illustration No. 18

Milan. Bobbin-made; continuous braid with brides; 17th–18th century

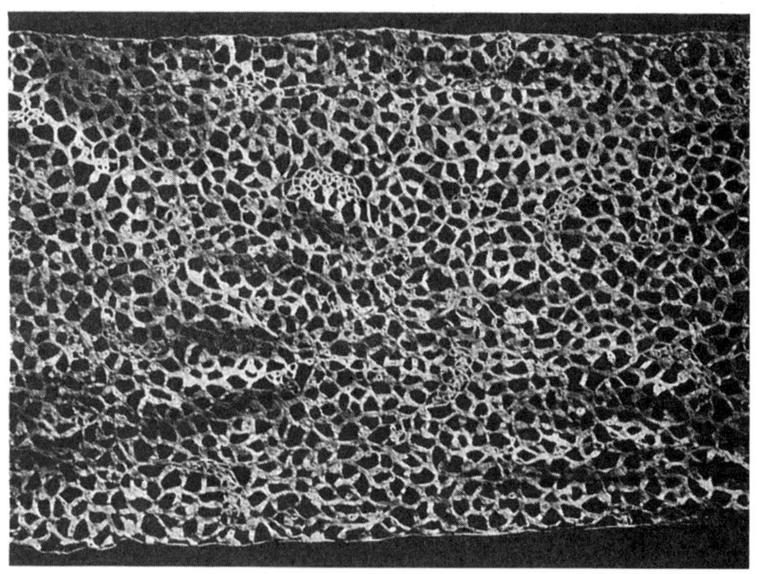

Illustration No. 19
Milan. Bobbin-made; continuous scroll; no foundation; 17th–18th century

solid part of bobbin lace as compared to the needle stitch in Venise.

The next step in Milan was the same tape-like design applied to a somewhat circular mesh ground, and with this came the freer use of "motifs," such as figures, animals, coats-of-arms, etc. By these various designs one can usually determine the century in which this lace was made, the more ornate and detailed the pattern, the later the period. Thus the scrolls and foliated designs of the Renaissance gave way to figures and flowers of the eighteenth century.

In all "Milan" lace the background or mesh was worked after the "motifs" (which were made separately and arranged in the desired pattern). The mesh is also bobbin-made and generally large and open.

There was a great demand for this lace owing to its adaptability to all ecclesiastical vestments, altar cloths, etc., which called for a durable and washable lace, but

Illustration No. 20

Milan. Bobbin-made; alb trimming on mesh foundation; 18th century

Illustration No. 21
Milan. Bobbin-made; continuous braid on mesh; 17th–18th century design with hunter and dog

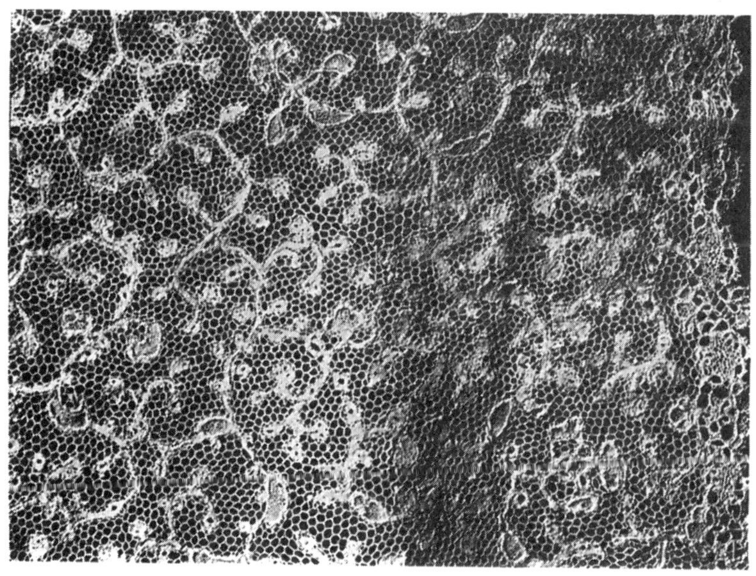

Illustration No. 22
Milan. Bobbin-made; continuous braid on mesh foundation; 18th century

unfortunately this very demand was the cause of the market being flooded with an inferior quality of this lace which, while resembling the other in pattern, was made with a bobbin-made tape that followed the design like an outline instead of making each "motif" on the pillow. This can readily be detected as the tape is either turned or gathered to fit the pattern, while otherwise

Illustration No. 23
Milan. Bobbin-made tape outlining design on mesh foundation; 18th century

the toilé would smoothly follow the curves of the pattern guided by the bobbin. There is probably a greater variety of Milan than almost any other lace, as it varies from the large flat, scrolling design with a great deal of toilé and no ground, to the similar design connected by "brides," then the small fine toilé with many brides, on to the later Milan, where the many motifs are joined by the large round mesh in its various degrees of quality.

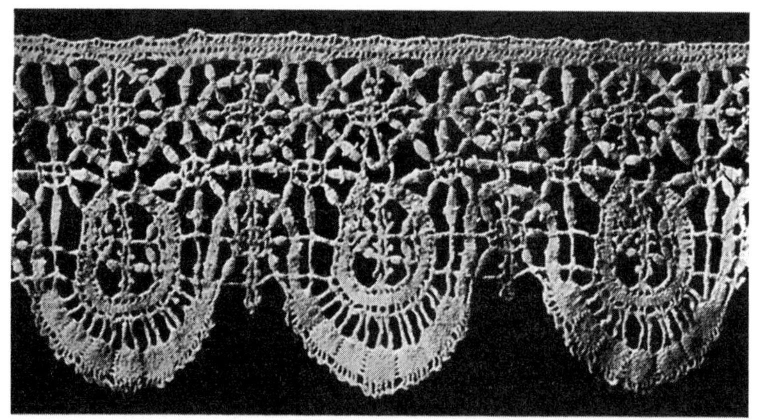

Illustration No. 24
Genoese. Bobbin-made Edge. First half of 17th century

Genoese—Point de Gênes

Although Italy is most famed for its two widely different types of lace represented by Venetian and Milanese, we must by no means ignore the work of the Genoese lace makers, who contributed so much to the lace industry of their country.

Like Milan this lace is made with the bobbin, although unlike the Milan it copies the design and patterns of the Venetian needle point. Its distinguishing feature, however, is the constant use of the flower design composed of petal-like "brides" in the shape of a cross within a circle and called the "Genoese Rose." This geometrical motif recurs constantly in the patterns and is easily recognizable. So skilful were the Genoese workers in imitating with their bobbins the early Venetian patterns found in the fifteenth and sixteenth century pattern books, that it is often only by close observation that they can be distinguished from the needle points of Venice.

The name of "point" incorrectly given to this bobbin-made lace undoubtedly originated from the fact that the best known laces of Genoa were made in deep points

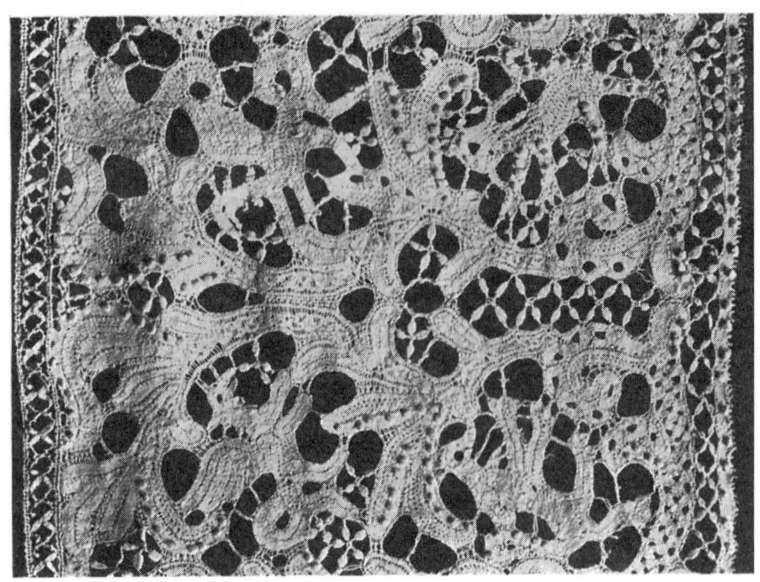

Illustration No. 25
Genoese. Bobbin-made; 18th century; showing "Genoese Rose"

and scallops as they were used to such a great extent for edging the ruffs and collars of the period.

Burano

We are putting Burano last in the list of Italian laces. not because it was the last to take up the industry, but rather because it is the one center which, right up to the present day has continued extensively the making

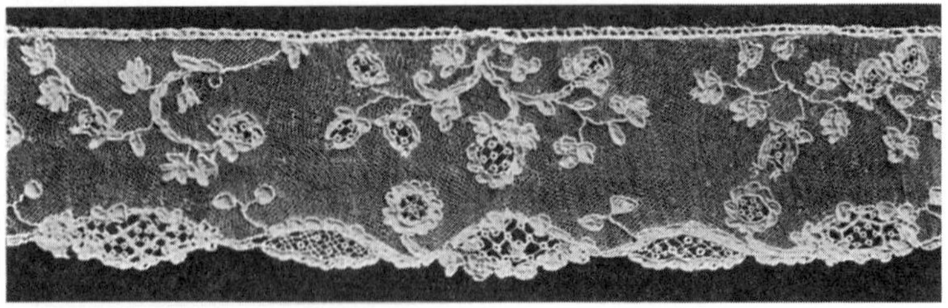

Illustration No. 26
Burano. Copy of Alençon; 18th century; showing streaky mesh

of lace, combining in its schools the reproducing of all types of lace, Italian, French and Flemish. These laces were made so skilfully as often to rival their models and defy detection by all save connoisseurs. The many laces such as Alençon and Argentan of the French and any number of the Flemish points are copied in great quantities. One distinguishing feature of the work of the Burano school is the cloudy, rather streaky effect of the mesh or réseau.

This réseau, which in the French and Flemish laces is clear and light, when compared to the Burano readily shows the difference of texture. This result is obtained by a certain method of throwing the thread to one side in a manner quite different from that done by the needle workers of other countries, and accounts for the perpendicular lined appearance of the mesh.

The name "Burano" does not apply to any one particular lace, as is the case with all other names, although

Illustration No. 27

Macramé. Border with bird design; 17th century

the Venise à Réseau or grounded Venise was generally accepted as being most characteristic of Burano.

Macramé

Before leaving the laces of Italy, it may be well to add a few words concerning a certain form of lace that is neither bobbin or needle, but made of the knotting of threads and known as Macramé.

This work is taught in the schools to a great extent and even in the poor houses, children of both sexes learn to make it. It is generally used as an edging for household linens and the long fringes of thread are usually knotted into rather geometrical designs. The ingenuity of the worker, however, often produces more novel and elaborate patterns.

Laces of Flanders

Before entering upon the description of the world-famous bobbin laces of Flanders, it seems to be the opportune moment to explain the meaning of the terms "Straight Lace" and "Free Lace."

Straight lace is the name given to the laces where the pattern and ground or réseau are made on the pillow at the same time, the bobbins following without interruption the pricked out design of "motif" and réseau. The laces made in this way are Valenciennes, Binche, Point de Paris, Lille, Malines, and all of the peasant laces of France and Italy.

On the other hand, "Free Lace" refers to the laces of which Point d'Angleterre, Honiton, Milan and Brussels are excellent examples.

The "motifs" in these laces are made separately, the réseau is worked afterwards and filled in around the pattern to which it is joined by means of a sort of slip stitch made by the bobbin with the aid of a sharp hook or pin called a "needle-pin." These two methods of making lace may be quite easily distinguished by looking closely to see whether the threads of the patterns continue in an unbroken line through to the réseau, or if they appear to end with the motif and begin again at another angle in the mesh; the former type is of course "straight lace," the latter "free."

Flemish

As we have already mentioned, lace-making started in Flanders about the same time as in Italy, but was almost exclusively bobbin in its early development. Flanders at once became one of the largest lace centers of the world and the marvelous skill and deftness of her workers made the industry a source of great wealth owing to the quantity of lace which she was able to export.

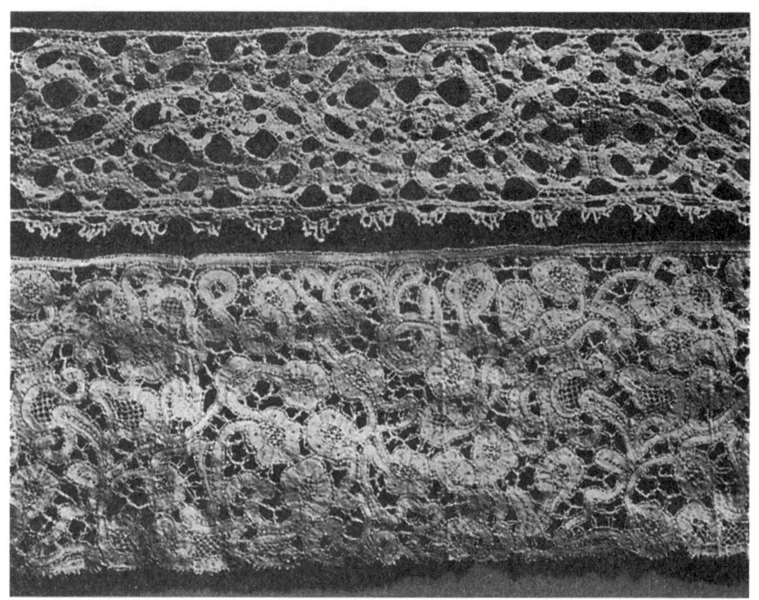

Illustration No. 28
Guipure de Flandre. 17th century

It is the exquisite fineness of the Flemish thread which has made her lace unequaled in quality and texture. The flax is spun in dark underground rooms to avoid contact with the dry air which might cause the thread to break, and it is this rare fineness which makes the "Vrai Réseau" or "Droschel" (as it is called in Flanders) so costly and inimitable.

It is also for this reason that regardless of the quantity of Flemish lace that was copied from the Spanish as well as Milanese patterns it is always distinguishable by a softness and fineness which is quite unlike the firm rather heavier texture of the Italian thread. There is also a slight difference in color, the thread being whiter in the Flemish than the Italian, which has a grayer tone.

Guipure

The earliest Flemish lace was known as Guipure, and like Milan it was a bobbin-made tape, the motifs of which in the early stages were joined by "brides," and in some cases only by the pattern itself. The designs of this lace, in the sixteenth and seventeenth centuries followed the Renaissance scrolls and foliated patterns of the period, the more elaborate flowers and figures coming later, as well as the use of the mesh.

Flemish Points

Flemish Points, wrongly named "Point," as they are bobbin-made laces, really include the laces of Bruges, Brussels (Brabant), and Point de Gênes. Calling it Point de Gênes has nothing to do with the Italian lace of that name, which was, as we said before, a bobbin-made copy of the Venetian needle point. But the Point de Gênes here referred to is actually Point de Flandre or Flemish Point.

There are great quantities of Flemish lace to be found, both very old and of more recent date, made in the various cities and provinces; these form a group in themselves, vast in number and difficult to describe save by illustrations, as they are mainly copies of the French, Italian and Spanish laces of the same type. Those, however, that have their distinctive characteristics and have acquired fame under their own name, instead of under the general classification of Flemish lace, are the following:

Mechlin (Malines)

Of all the Flemish laces, Malines or Mechlin (which is the English term) is the daintiest and airiest. It is a "straight" lace, and owing to the fact that it was used mainly for the trimming of personal attire it was rarely made as wide as the other Flemish laces. Its distinguishing feature is the cordonnet or flat silky thread that outlines the pattern. The beautiful light mesh is hexagonal in shape, being made by the twisting twice of two threads on four sides and plaiting four threads three times on the other two sides.

The very free use of the silk thread outline is an unfailing guide to Mechlin, as it almost always appears

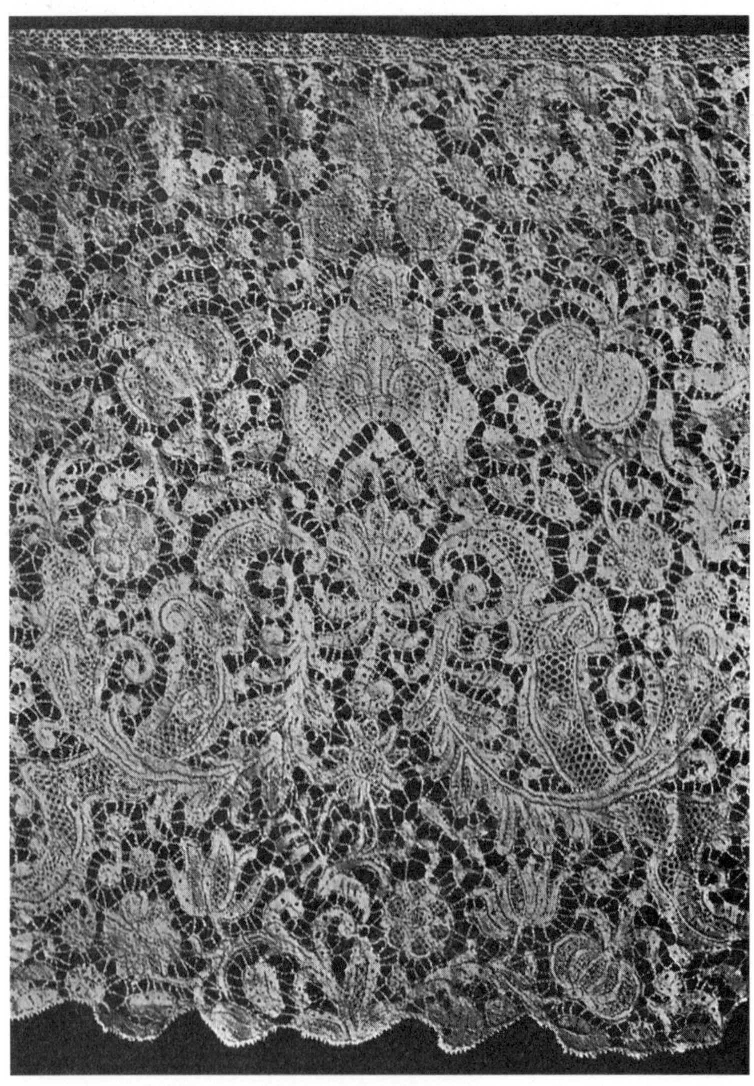

Illustration No. 29

"Point de Flandre." With brides; 18th century

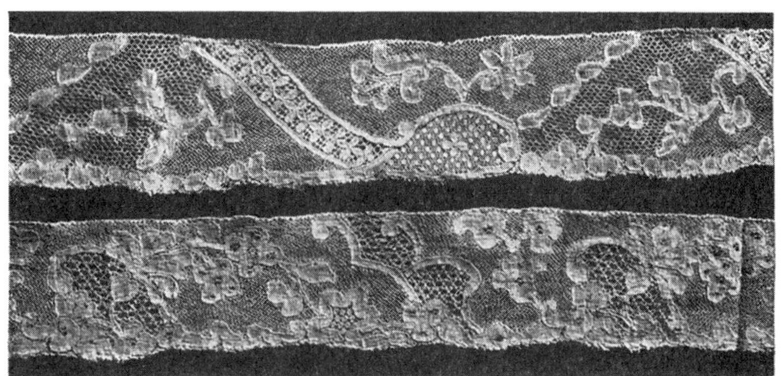

Illustration No. 30
Mechlin, or Malines. First half of 18th century
Showing réseau rosacé

in this lace in a greater or less degree. Were it not for this, it would often be confused with "Angleterre" despite the fact that the latter is a "free" lace.

Malines of the seventeenth and early eighteenth century shows the large flowery spray and inserted openwork stitches known variously as "œil de perdrix," "fond de neige," "réseau-rosacé," etc., and having very little of the plain mesh. It is similar in design and composition to the Angleterre of the same period. With the advance of the eighteenth century Malines became lighter and filmier, characterized now by a great deal of soft, simple mesh, ornamented now and then with little dots or "point d'esprit," and having the small bouquet of flowers at the very edge of the lace. It became very popular at the French court and it was its charming adaptability to the fashion of the day that made Malines the lace of frills and furbelows.

Antwerp

We take occasion here to mention Antwerp on account of a certain familiar type of lace made there. It was used by the women as an edging for their caps and called "Potten Kant," or "pot lace," so named on account of the design, which was a basket or pot from

Illustration No. 31
Malines Handkerchief. Eighteenth century

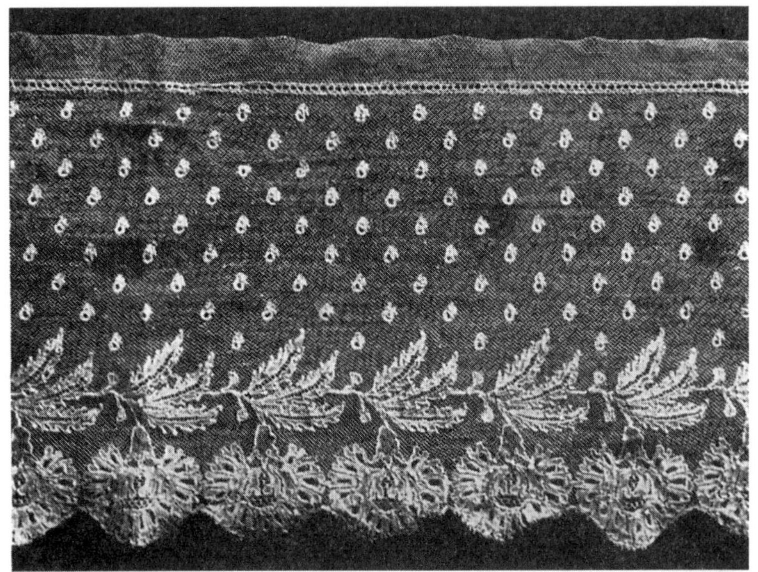

Illustration No. 32
Malines. Late 18th century; with "point d'esprit"

which sprang rather conventional flowers. It is often said that this "motif" represents the "lily of annunciation," and is seen reproduced in many other laces. In quality and appearance it is a cross between Binche and Mechlin, having the ground of the former, and the silky outline of the latter.

Angleterre

The laces that have become known to us under the name of Point d'Angleterre are very varied. This is due mainly to the fact that in the year 1662, in order to stimulate the home industry, an English edict was passed prohibiting the importation of foreign-made laces. This would have meant a great loss to Flanders, so nothing daunted, she immediately renamed the laces made for the English market, putting them all under the head of "Point d'Angleterre" or "English Point." Through this deception she was able to sell her laces to England.

While in the beginning this name was applied to a great many Brussels laces it gradually settled down as a term of its own and became famous as one of the most elaborate and beautiful of the Flemish laces. Although even up to the present time it is better known as Point d'Angleterre, it is frequently called "Old Brussels Point," though I feel that the latter term is somewhat confusing, owing to the fact that there is a more modern *needle*-made lace named Brussels Point. The early lace of this type closely resembles the Mechlin, as we already mentioned, the main difference being in the absence of the silk thread outline and in the formation of the mesh, which though of the same airy type is a little more oblong or lozenge shape, due to the use of an extra plait on either side. This mesh, the famous "Vrai Réseau," or "Droschel," was made in narrow strips, about an inch wide and joined together by means of a stitch called "point de raccroc" or "fine joining."

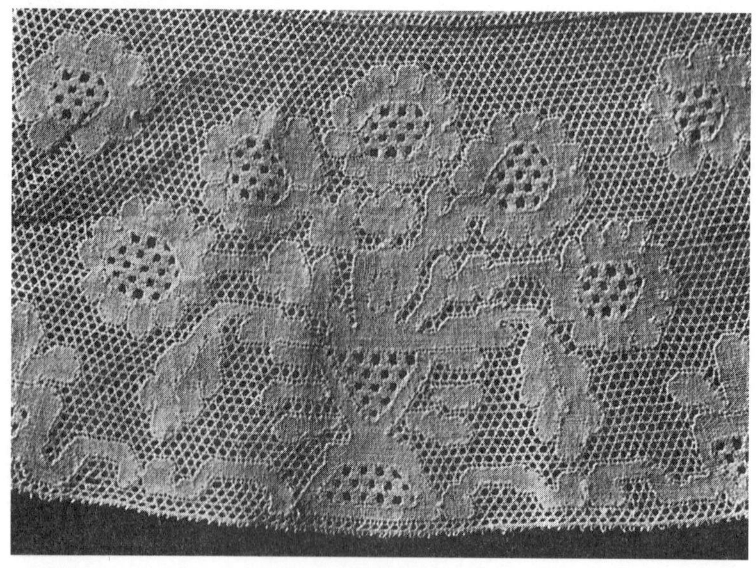

Illustration No. 33
Antwerp. Potten Kant; 17th–18th century

Illustration No. 34
"Point d'Angleterre." Clear example of cote around design and with variety of grounds

Angleterre is a "free lace" and the slightly raised edge or "cote" around the flowers and motifs is very characteristic, and gives a beautiful effect of relief.

Illustration No. 35

"Point d'Angleterre." With brides. End of 17th century

Illustration No. 36

"Point d'Angleterre." Louis XV; corner of square showing use of Chinese figures in design

As is true of nearly all lace, there are many distinctly varying types of "Angleterre," influenced naturally by the designs of the period in which they were made as well as by the quality of workmanship.

The earlier type of about the seventeenth century was the conventional style of the period, which showed itself in other laces, namely, large scrolls and motifs joined by "brides." Then came the net background which generally has the large bold flowers and rather open mesh left by the pattern in wide patches. This is probably the least attractive of the many types of Angleterre, as it seems to lack the daintiness and beauty of design so

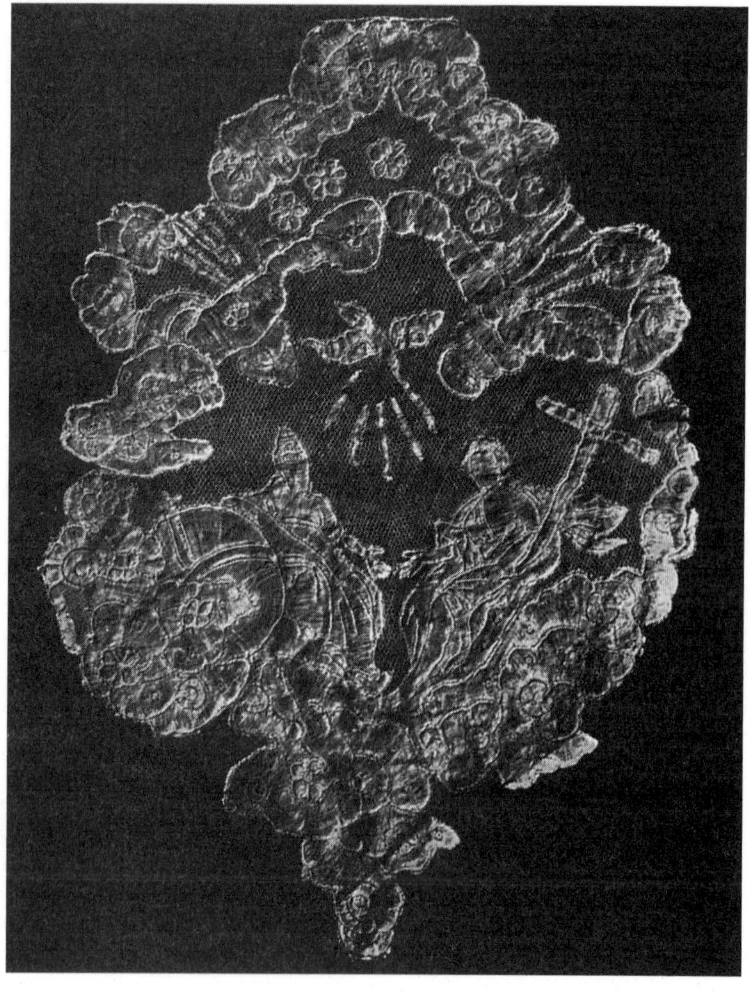

Illustration No. 37

"Point d'Angleterre." On mesh; 18th century; center of chalice veil

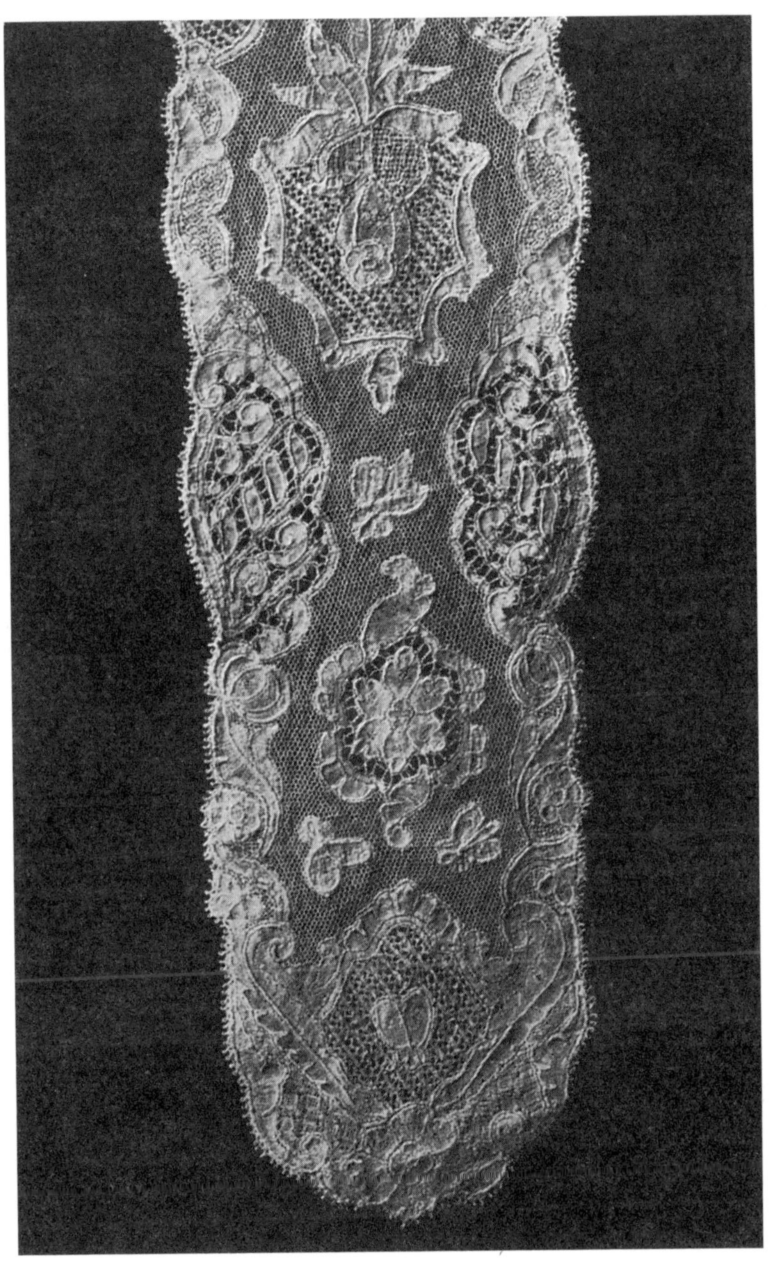

Illustration No. 38
"Point d'Angleterre." On mesh; 18th century lappet

characteristic of this lace. Next came the finer workmanship and more graceful and elaborate designs of the eighteenth century, showing the fine sheer réseau, which was soon to attain a delicacy comparable only to a spider's web, and exquisite flowers and figures of the most delicate texture.

Last, but not least, we now come to the very finest of all the Angleterre points. This is the type, which has neither the mesh ground or the connecting "brides," the motifs of the pattern coming directly together. It is only a close inspection of this lace which will show to the best advantage the marvelous skill of the fingers that plied their bobbins to produce the myriad stitches employed in fashioning the bouquets and other elaborate designs, such as vases, urns, "lilies of the annunciation," etc. The whole piece when finished has the appearance of a filmy bit of fabric, so close are the motifs and so sheer and fine the toilé. The "fond de neige," used to a great extent in this kind of Angleterre, has, as the name implies, the appearance of snowflakes, so round and fluffy are the tiny discs which are dotted together in small groups. There is another well-known "fond" common to these laces called "œil de perdrix," which so closely resembles the "fond de neige" that they are practically the same, with the exception of the small hole in the center of the mesh design.

Binche

We now come to the third of the trio of beautiful Flemish laces, namely, Malines, Angleterre, and Binche.

Binche is quite unlike the other two in appearance as the réseau is much heavier and more solid in texture, having a somewhat honey-combed effect, obtained by plaiting the threads in such a manner as to form a small, rather solid square with five tiny holes, and called "fond à la vierge," or "cinq trous." This mesh is distinctly

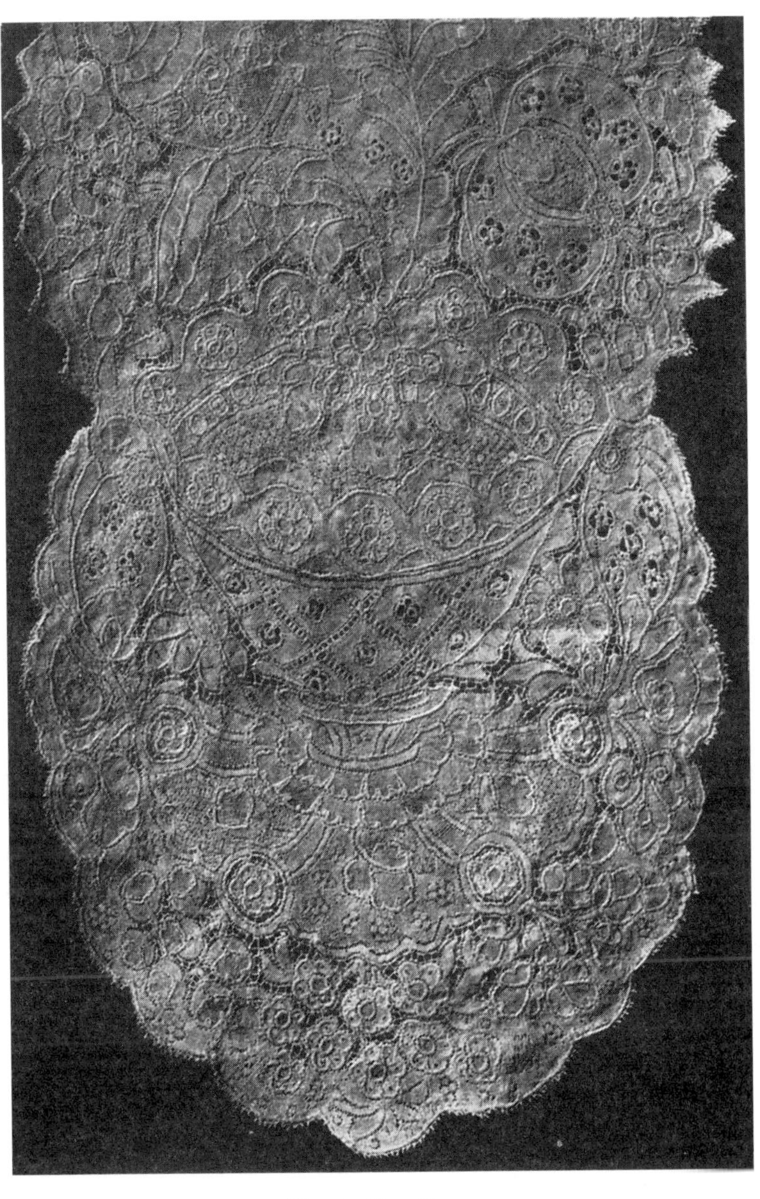

Illustration No. 39
"Point d'Angleterre." Eighteenth century barbe; no mesh; great variety of grounds

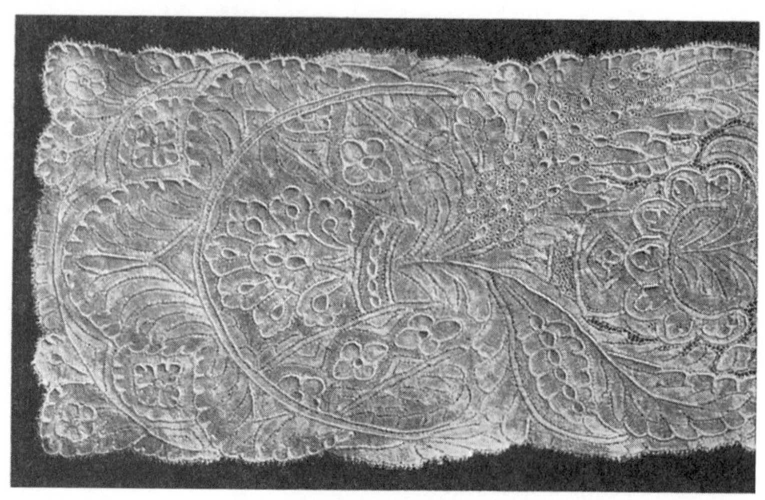

Illustration No. 40

"Point d'Angleterre." Eighteenth century barbe; fine example of cote around motifs

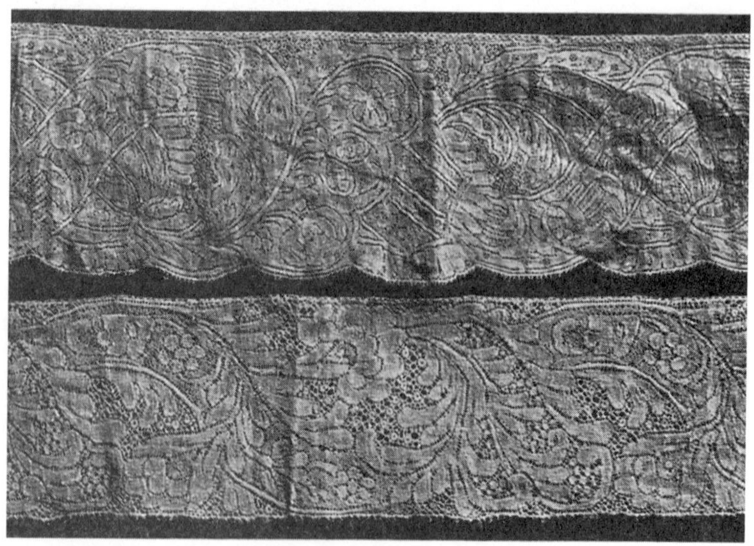

Illustration No. 41

Binche or Fausse Valenciennes. End of 17th century

characteristic as it is rarely or never found in any other lace.

The early Binche of the seventeenth century, so closely resembles the Valenciennes of the same period that it is often called "Fausse Valenciennes." This type has no réseau, is extremely light and delicate and has the filmy effect obtained by the very sheer toilé. The "fond de neige" which we have already mentioned in

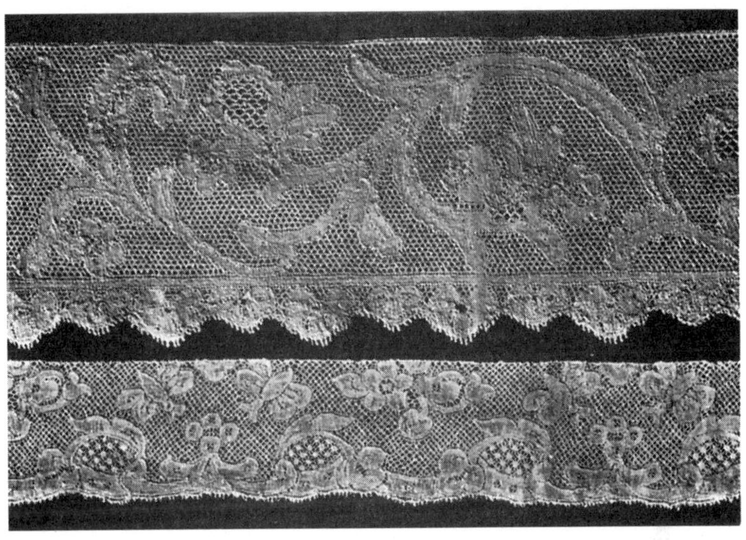

Illustration No. 42
Binche. With "cinq-trous fond"; 18th century

connection with Angleterre is used a great deal in Binche and is in fact one of the few stitches which distinguishes it from Valenciennes as the latter seldom has this particular "fond."

As time advanced Binche acquired a greater amount of réseau, which makes it familiar to us now and also the use of a thin thread outline somewhat resembling Mechlin, around the "motifs." This is the type that is imitated at the present time in such great quantities in machine-made lace.

Illustration No. 43
Duchesse. End of 18th century

"Duchesse" or Bruges

Duchesse, the least attractive of the Flemish laces, is really a combination of the "motifs" of several types of lace, and rather resembles the sprigs of Honiton joined by brides, or even Guipure de Flandre. The name Duchesse is a modern term for this type of Flemish bobbin lace, which in its early development was known as Guipure de Bruges.

Brussels Point à l'Aiguille or Point de Gaze

We now come down to the most modern of the Flemish laces known as Brussels "Point à l'Aiguille," or "Point de Gaze."

Its particular interest lies not merely in the fact that it is the only needle-point lace of Flanders to attain fame; but also because of its great popularity in all countries, during the nineteenth century, right up to the present time. Due to its adaptability to personal adornment, in the way of wedding veils, scarfs and dress trimming of all kinds, it was made in great quan-

Illustration No. 44
Brussels "Point à l'Aiguille" or "Point de Gaze"; 19th century

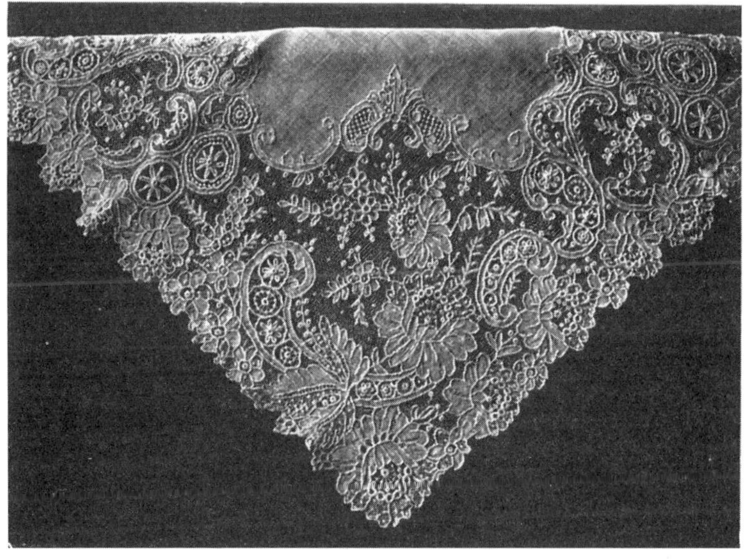

Illustration No. 45
Brussels "Point à l'Aiguille" or "Point de Gaze" Handkerchief. Nineteenth century

tities and attained a perfection of workmanship that places it among the most elaborate as well as skilful examples of needle-point lace. The frequent appearance of the rose in the design is responsible for the term "Rose Point," so often used today.

Point de Gaze is made on the finest of needle meshes, the magnificent bouquets and floral designs reflecting the ornate taste of the nineteenth century. These sprigs are made at the same time as the mesh and joined by fine stitches which are concealed by leaves and sprays. Unlike the needle laces of Alençon and Argentan there is no raised buttonhole, only a thread outline around the motifs. A curious and attractive effect of shading the flowers is obtained by part of the toilé being made of a solid stitch and part of an open stitch.

Laces of France

Although the Italian wife of Henry II, Catharine de Medici, in 1545 introduced lace-making into France, the industry in both Italy and Flanders was well established before France entered the field as a rival. It was through the untiring efforts of Louis XIV's clever and ambitious Minister Colbert that in 1665 the first school of lace was opened in France.

It was to the little town of Alençon that he brought Italy's most skilled lace makers, paying them lavishly to teach his countrywomen their perfected art, in order that France, too, might produce lace which would equal in beauty those that she was buying in such great quantities from both Italy and Flanders.

The time was most propitious for such a venture, the reign of "Le Roi Soleil," patron of all the arts, was limitless in its extravagance. Men and women of the court as well as prelates of the Church, adorned themselves with the most luxuriant laces. It was a natural sequence that the industry should quickly establish itself, not only having the protection of the powerful minister but being also greatly favored by the fashion of the day. Well-known artists vied with each other in making designs to be executed by both needle and bobbin, so that France in a few short years was able to equal, and in some cases excel, her rivals.

It was quite to be expected that France with her great creative genius, so well exemplified in all her artistic achievements, should produce a lace that would become world-famous for its beauty of design and workmanship.

Point de France

In bringing over the Italian workers it was natural that the earliest type of lace produced by the French schools should have been an exact reproduction of the laces of Italy. Owing to the enormous popularity of the beautiful Venetian points their first efforts were turned toward copying these laces, and so well did they do it that to this day there is difficulty in distinguishing them.

The heavy Guipure or Venetian Gros Point was made first and renamed in France "Point Colbert," in honor of its patron. In fact, as soon as the industry acquired a footing, a royal edict demanded that all needle lace made in France should be known as "Point de France."

This, of course, has caused much discussion in later years as to the real origin of many laces. Needless to say, the quantities of needle point lace turned out in the style and quality of the Venetian points has necessitated marking many pieces of lace seen in museums and collections: "Point de Venise" or "Point de France." This is true mainly of the lace produced in the reign of Louis XIV, for already with the beginning of Louis XV the creative spirit of the French designers had improved on their models, embellishing them with many extra touches, birds, animals, fountains and Chinese figures, not to be found in the more classical designs of the Italian points. Thus, the trained eye of the connoisseur can readily attribute these laces to

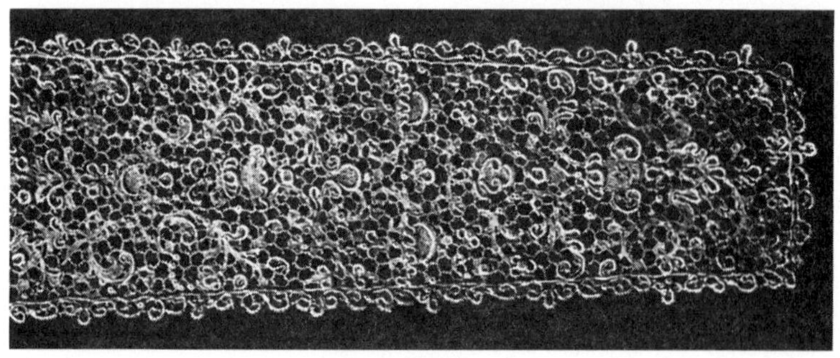

Illustration No. 46
"Point de France" or "Point de Venise." Seventeenth century lappet

Illustration No. 47
"Point de France" Chalice Veil. Eighteenth century; showing elaborate design

France, although in texture and execution they are identical with those made in Italy.

Alençon

Although we have just mentioned that it was in the town of Alençon that Point de France had its origin, the name, today, typifies quite a different lace. The lessons they learnt from the Italian lace makers taught the women of Alençon to become very skilful with their needles, and they soon began to imitate the Venetian patterns. The result was a needle point lace whose delicacy of design as well as washable and durable qualities have given it an enviable place amongst the beautiful laces of the world.

Alençon is made on a fine needle point réseau, made by twisting several threads together and giving the mesh a hexagonal shape. The patterns are usually bouquets or single flowers like carnations and roses, besides the undulating ribbon of the Louis XV period. During the period of Louis XVI the ground was often dotted or "semé" with tiny flowers, pods, or dots and even, under Napoleon, with bees, still retaining the rather elaborate border effect of the earlier laces. These flowers are made with the use of a cordonnet outline obtained by placing a horse hair around all the flowers and motifs, and buttonholing over them, often adding tiny "picots" besides.

We are told that, with the exception of Argentan, this is the only lace in which the use of horse hair may

Illustration No. 48

Alençon. Eighteenth century; with carnation pattern and elaborate needle point stitches

Illustration No. 49
Alençon. Louis XVI
A—Veil with mesh semé with tiny pods
B—Border showing combination of heavy and fine mesh

be found, and it is to this that the pattern owes its decided effect of relief. A variety of intricate needle stitches are also used in the pattern and it was the

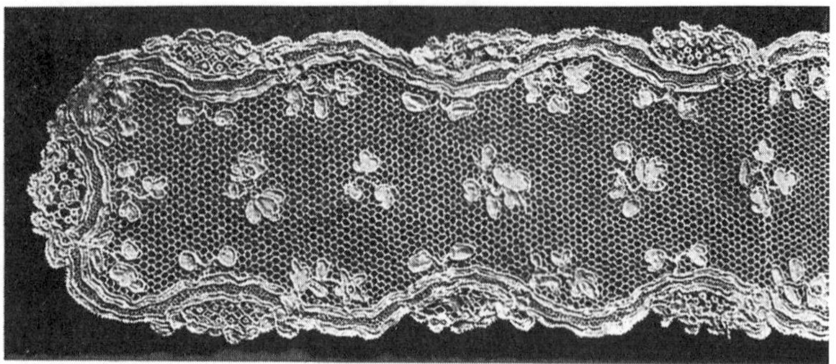

Illustration No. 50
Argentan. Eighteenth century lappet; hexagonal button-holed mesh

readiness with which Alençon lent itself to the ruffles, jabots and "fontanges" of the day that it became a favorite with the ladies of the court.

Argentan

The neighboring town of Argentan produced at the same time a lace so identical with Alençon as to be prac-

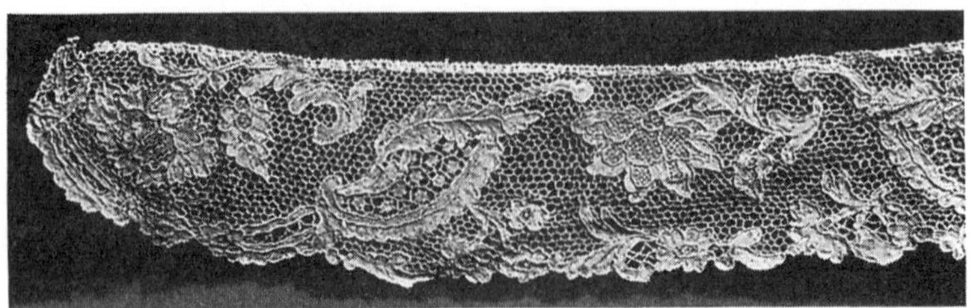

Illustration No. 51
Argentan. Eighteenth century

tically indistinguishable. The quality and texture of the needle point was alike, and the same designs were copied in both towns. One way, however, to distinguish them is to closely examine the mesh. The réseau in Argentan is hexagonal in shape like the Alençon, but was *button-holed* instead of *twisted.* Naturally this may be quickly detected in the large flounces or on pieces of less good quality where both mesh and pattern are coarser, but, in the fine light laces with the réseau of minute workmanship, it is difficult to see.

We now leave the needle point laces of France, and while they are only three in number—Point de France, Alençon, and Argentan—they play a very important part in the beautiful laces of the world, both in quality

Illustration No. 52
Valenciennes. Seventeenth century; resembling Binche

and quantity, owing to the fact that the enormous demand was caused by the style of dress of the period, both for men and women. The paintings of the eighteenth century, in their minute detail of dress and furnishings, give us ample proof of the many uses these laces were put to, during the reigns of Louis XV and Louis XVI.

Valenciennes

Valenciennes is a small town in the north, almost as much Flemish as French, so much so, in fact, that the lace of this name is as often claimed by Flanders as by

Illustration No. 53
Valenciennes. Eighteenth century

France. This bobbin-made lace was to become probably the most popular and well known of all laces.

The Valenciennes of the seventeenth century was quite different from the lace of that name we know today. In speaking of Binche we referred to the fact that the early lace of that type was so often confused with the Valen-

Illustration No. 54
Valenciennes. Eighteenth century

ciennes that the lace not actually made in the town of Valenciennes became known as "Fausse Valenciennes," or Binche. Some authorities claim that there is a slight distinction, namely that the free use of the "fond de neige" is typical of Binche, while rarely appearing in Valenciennes, otherwise the pattern and execution of the two laces are identical, and there are even conflicting opinions on this minor detail. From this came the well-known "Val," so famous today, that is, the type with a great deal of réseau and a scattered floral design. Valenciennes is a "straight" lace, the work all being made in one piece, generally in narrow widths, for deep

Illustration No. 55
A—Ave Maria edge
B—"Point de Dieppe"; resembling Valenciennes

flounces of this lace are seldom seen, as it was rarely used in trimming of church vestments. The réseau or ground is made in several different ways, the earlier having the small round mesh, heavily plaited, not much in use at present. Later, a square or diamond mesh of the same type took its place. Valenciennes is said to be the most difficult of all laces to make, notwithstanding its apparent simplicity. This is due, not only to the many ways of making the ground but also to the texture and fineness of the toilé. The designs are more or less

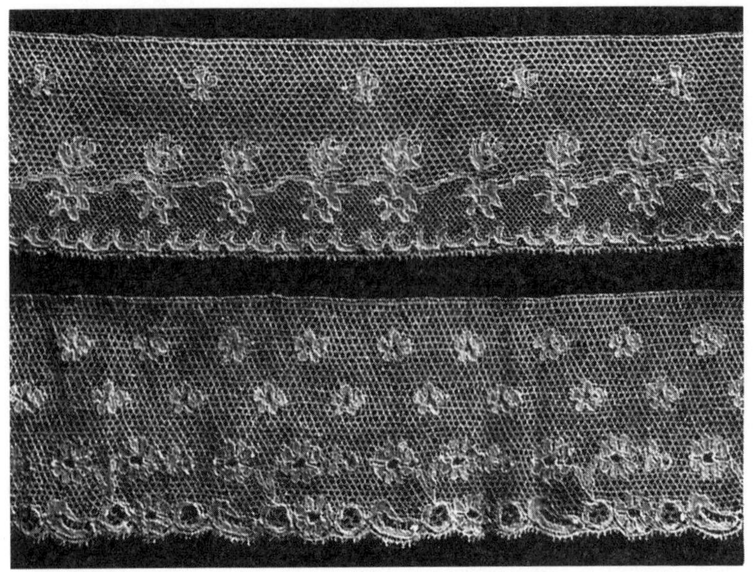

Illustration No. 56
"Point de Paris." Nineteenth century; showing six-pointed star mesh

conventional, with a great deal of plain réseau and the motifs of carefully drawn flowers, such as roses, tulips, leaves, etc., appearing near the edge of the lace.

There are two narrow unimportant laces often called Valenciennes, which are in reality "Point de Dieppe" and "Ave Maria." Both were made in the town of Dieppe, where Valenciennes of an inferior quality is also made in great quantities today.

Point de Paris

Point de Paris is a light bobbin lace made with the famous "fond chant," or six-pointed star, mesh. It is similar to Valenciennes in design, but having a thread outline around the pattern.

Lille

The northern town of Lille, which, like Valenciennes, was claimed equally by France and Flanders, produced a great deal of lace, both black and white. Lille is a

Illustration No. 57
Lille. Eighteenth century; showing "fond simple"

Illustration No. 58
Lille. Nineteenth century; with "point d'esprit"

"straight" lace, having a very simple réseau known as the "fond clair" or "fond simple," and, being the lightest and most transparent of the bobbin-made grounds, the motifs are outlined with a silky thread, resembling Malines. The earlier patterns are stiff and the edges straight, while the later designs are more ornate and the "point d'esprit" on the mesh is frequently introduced. This lace is also made in large quantities today and is copied to a great extent in machine-made laces.

Illustration No. 59
Chantilly Handkerchief. Eighteenth century

Chantilly

Chantilly, which gives its name to a beautiful lace, was a wide center of lace-making—some hundred towns, all following the same industry. Chantilly was not made as early as some of the other laces and came into vogue only during the reign of Louis XVI, reaching the height of its popularity about 1830.

While lace known as Spanish Blonde was also made at Chantilly, it is for the black silk lace that the name is justly famed. The flowers and ground are of the same silk, the cordonnet being a thicker thread, flat and untwisted. The stitches used in the motifs of Chantilly were made up of the earlier mesh grounds such as "cinq-trous," "fond de mariage," etc. The black Chantilly lace, which has the appearance of thread, is really made of a grenadine silk, which, owing to its lack of luster, is often mistaken for thread. The distinguishing feature is the "fond chant," or six-pointed star, mesh, of the earlier Chantilly, the lace of the last century often having the hexagonal ground of the Alençon. It was made up into scarfs, mantillas and parasols of the period, and the elaborateness of the floral designs made it very popular for export to Spain and her American colonies.

There were countless little towns in France that made

Illustration No. 60

A—Cluny

B—Torchon

lace that bore their names, but it is needless to enumerate them here as they varied but little and can readily come under the head of those laces that we have already named.

Cluny and Torchon

These laces, made with a very coarse thread, are produced in great quantities today in France for the trimming of household linens.

We trust now, to have touched on all the laces of importance belonging to the three countries that have played so great a part in the lace-making of the world. Italy, Flanders, and France have given us the priceless examples of needle and bobbin laces, which by their unexcelled workmanship have reflected the talent, fashion and luxury of three centuries.

Laces of Spain

Early lace-making in Spain was contemporaneous with Italy and Flanders. She copied the needle points of Italy and the bobbin laces of Flanders, but her greatest achievement was the production of the gold and silver as well as colored thread lace, worn so much by the Spanish grandees, and imported into France under Louis XIV, and which attained international fame under the name of "Point d'Espagne."

The national mantilla was, of course, a large product of their bobbins and a great variety of qualities and styles were produced. Many of the bobbin laces of Spain are characterized by the use of the lily and pomegranate, symbols of the cities of Seville and Granada as well as the moresque designs copied from the work of the Moors and distinguished by the lack of any save geometrical patterns, the use of figures, animals, etc., being forbidden by the Mohammedan religion.

Spanish Blonde

The lace principally associated with Spain today is what is known as "Blonde," although as we have just said, she made great quantities of bobbin lace in imitation of the coarser types of Flemish and Italian.

The Blonde is used mainly for the mantillas and scarfs worn by the women of Spain, and, strange to say, it seems to be among the few styles that have remained unchanged through the varying fashions of other countries. We always picture the Spanish woman in her mantilla of black or white Blonde, often accompanied by an over-skirt of fine Chantilly.

The Blonde lace, either white or black, is generally made of silk, in the large floral designs so distinctly Spanish. A great deal of this lace is made today on a machine net, the bobbin flowers worked in and outlined with a heavy silk thread run in with a needle. On the

Illustration No. 61
Spanish Blonde. Eighteenth century

other hand, however, when the machine net is not used, it is a "straight lace," réseau and motifs being made at the same time. The white lace is seen in several tones, the creamy being the familiar Blonde, while that having a silvery sheen is known as "Silver Blonde."

Appliqué

We are taking this opportunity to mention the Appliqué or Applied lace. It belongs more to modern times, as it was only after the machine net came into use, less than a hundred years ago, that it was made to any extent. The wide machine mesh lent itself readily to the making of wedding veils and wide flounces and even entire dresses upon which were applied both needle and bobbin-made motifs. We come across some examples of the "Vrai Réseau" among the old laces of Flanders, France and England, but as is readily understood, there

Illustration No. 62
Appliqué. Nineteenth century

was no real advantage in applying the flowers to a hand-made réseau, it being just as easy to make both mesh and motif together as in any "straight" lace. The advantage of Appliqué lay in the saving of time and expense by making great quantities of net on the machine and then sewing on the hand-made flowers which could be made in detached sprays of either flowers or leaves by various workers and then assembled for final application in the main work-room.

It seems barely necessary to say that to distinguish Appliqué, all one need do is to look on the wrong side of the lace to see that the motifs are sewn or applied to the

Illustration No. 63
Appliqué Scarf. Eighteenth century; on "vrai réseau" showing lines where mesh was joined

Illustration No. 64
Filet. Buratto. Sixteenth century; mesh made with two threads down and one across

mesh, the net in most cases being left on the back of the pattern.

Filet

The making of Filet, or Lacis, as it is often called, was contemporaneous with the early drawn work and it continued in its original type down through the centuries to the present day. It was the favorite pastime of queens and ladies of the court, and vast quantities in squares and strips were produced in the sixteenth and seventeenth centuries. Legend tells us that Catherine de Medici alone had more than five hundred of these squares of her own making, in her lace chests. Filet was comparatively easy to make and most effective as a trimming for altar cloths and household linens.

The famous pattern books of the fifteenth and sixteenth centuries, such as those of Parasole and Vinciolo, were designed, to a great extent, for the Filet or Lacis, and strange to say, the patterns seen and made today vary little from these original designs.

There are two different types of Filet, one where the mesh is plain and the pattern worked in with a linen

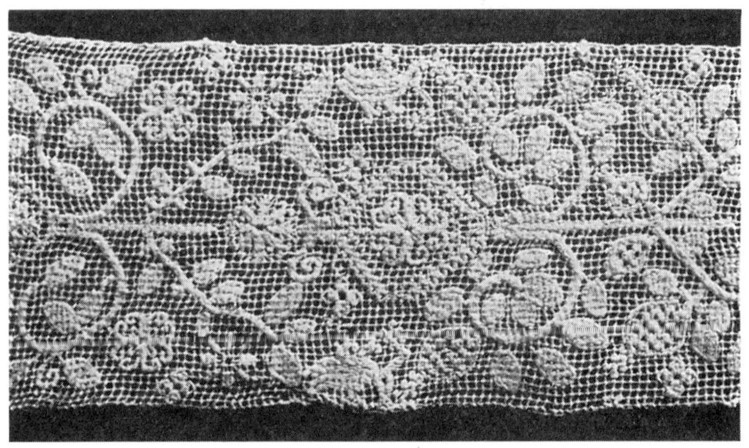

Illustration No. 65

Filet. Lacis. Seventeenth century; knotted mesh and darning stitch

Illustration No. 66
Filet. Modern type

stitch, giving an almost woven appearance to the design and known as Buratto. The other, where the mesh is knotted and the design worked in with a regular darning stitch, or Point de Reprise, is called Lacis. This lace was generally made in rather wide flounces and strips as well as the squares mentioned before, and with a coarse thread, as it was so often used in conjunction with heavy linen; it is only today that it is made in narrow edges and insertions, with a finer linen thread. The Filet of the present day comes more under the head of lace than the original work so called, for it was really, up to the middle of the nineteenth century, more of an embroidery than a lace.

Laces of England

In England as in other countries lace-making has a very hazy origin. Records show us that lace or something very much like it was made about the same time as elsewhere, but it was really not until the reign of Henry VIII that it attained national interest under the patronage of Katharine of Aragon, who possibly brought from her native country, Spain, a greater fondness for lace than had been previously displayed by any of the English queens. All things pertaining to fashion or wearing apparel can be easily brought to the fore if favored by royalty, and it was no doubt the fashion of the large ruffs that were in vogue then and worn both by men and women that called for more and more lace.

We said, at the beginning, that we would touch but lightly on English laces, for while the industry was very

Illustration No. 67

Buckinghamshire. *A*—Back of lady's cap; eighteenth century
B—Nineteenth century edge; like Lille

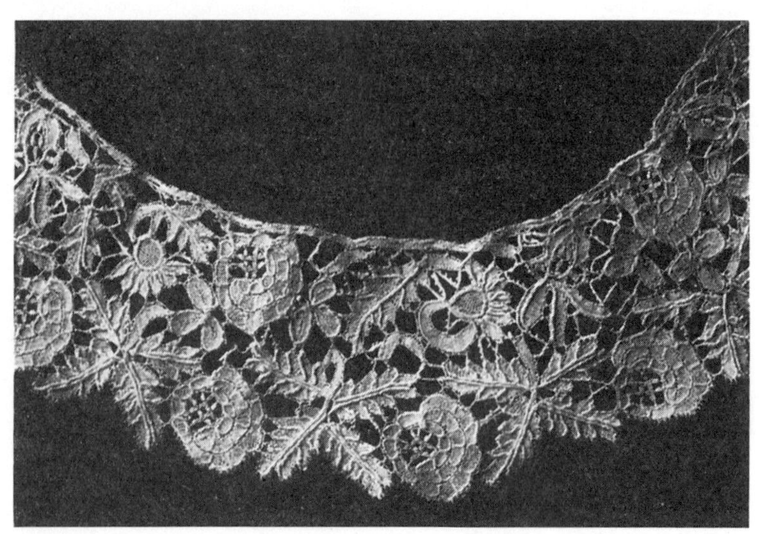

Illustration No. 68
Honiton Guipure. Collar; 19th century

Illustration No. 69
Honiton. Applied to hand-made mesh

much developed and great quantities of lace produced, the creative spirit was wanting and the lace made in England lacked the individuality of that made in other countries. In other words, all kinds were made in England, but none of them were typically English as were the Venetians and Milans typical of Italy, Alençon and Point de France of France and Flemish Points of Flanders.

She produced in later times laces more on the style of Brussels or Flemish and those of northern France, such as Lille, etc., which are called Devonshire, Buckinghamshire, etc. The accompanying illustrations will readily show their characteristics better than any word description.

These laces are so well copied by the machine that it is often difficult to tell them apart.

Honiton is a much used lace today, and is probably more typically English than any of the others, and as it was generally made in Devonshire, it is also known by that name.

Laces of Ireland

Ireland, too, had her laces, and they need no introduction, for they are probably the one type familiar to all.

The laces that we have hitherto described belong either to bobbin or needle, but Irish lace established a new class and shows us what beautiful effects may be obtained by the use of the crochet hook. When crochet

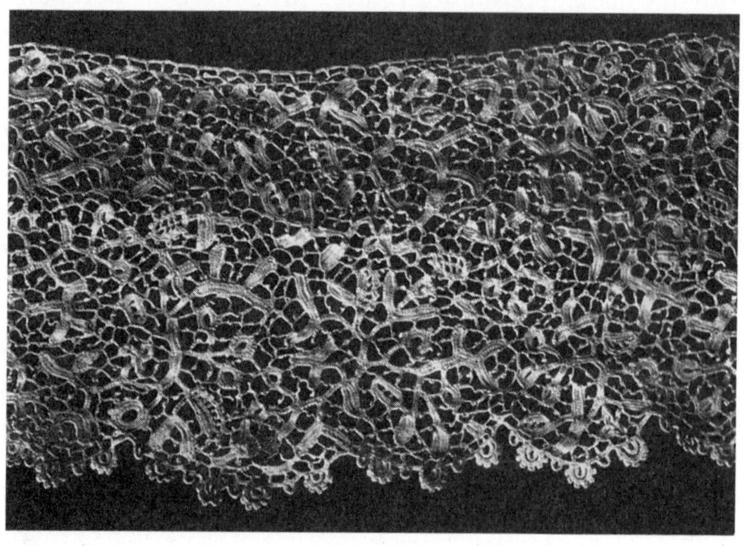

Illustration No. 70
Irish Crochet. Imitating Venetian needle point; 19th century

lace-making first started, about 1850, in the convents of Ireland, the nuns turned their first efforts to copying, as closely as the crochet stitch permitted, the Venetian needle point. This accounts for the remarkable similarity of some of the fine, earlier pieces of Irish to the Point de Venise. The nuns soon began to perfect their own designs, however, and produced the patterns which have become known the world over as Irish crochet.

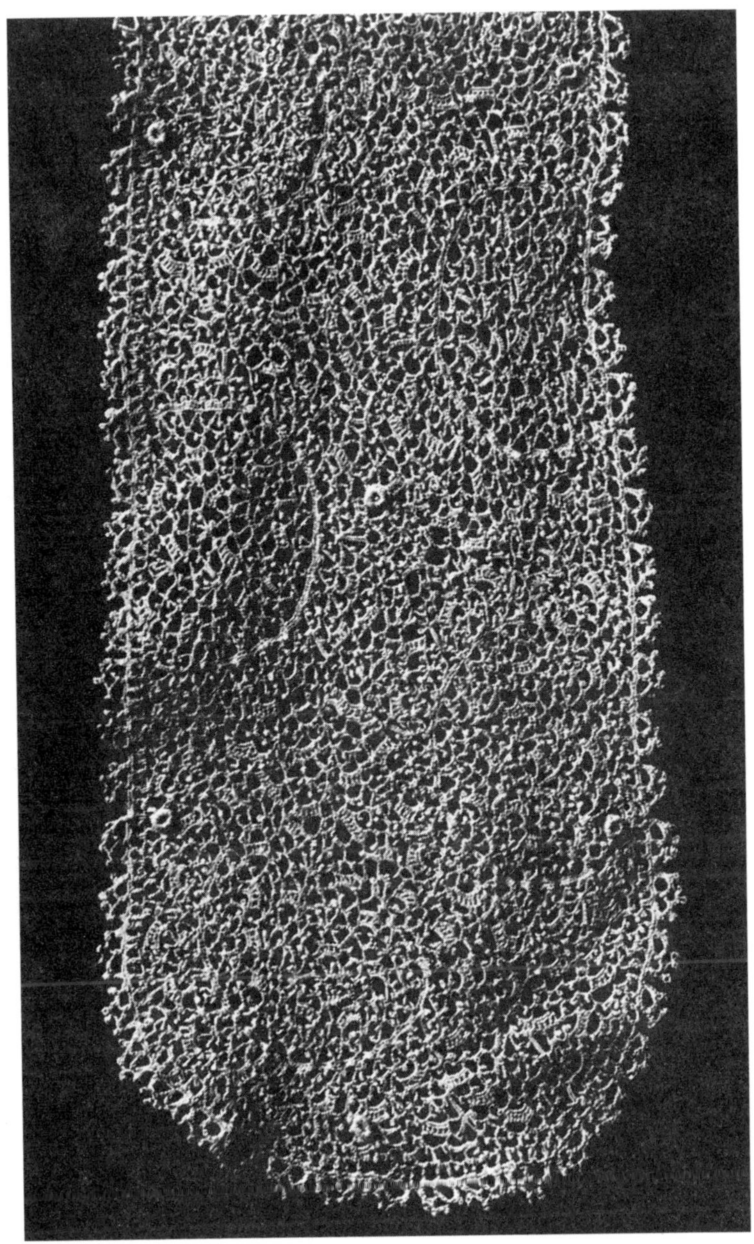

Illustration No. 71

Irish Crochet. Nineteenth century; barbe; rare specimen of fine old crochet

Illustration No. 72
Irish Crochet. Modern type of fine and heavy stitch

It seems barely necessary to describe this lace, as its great popularity, during the last half of the nineteenth century has made it famous.

Irish lace is copied today in many countries, all of whom turn out a very good imitation of this crochet; but owing to a certain quality and color of her thread as well as the dexterity of workmanship and a method of starching, Ireland still holds supremacy in the making of real Irish crochet. It may be of interest to add that the making of this lace is today part of the education of the children in convents and schools, and the industry forms quite a monetary asset to the Emerald Isle.

Limerick

Several other laces besides crochet are made in Ireland, among which the Limerick or Tambour lace is well known. This lace, which derives its name from the tambourine-shaped frame on which the net is stretched, is made by drawing the thread through the mesh with a hooked needle to form the design.

Needle run lace is of a similar type, the thread, however, being finer and run in with a needle instead of drawn in with a tambour. These laces are very machine-like in appearance.

Carrickmacross

Carrickmacross, the making of which was started about 1820, and was the earliest Irish lace industry, is really made by a design cut out of a thin white cambric, appliquéd on to a net with point stitches and outlined with a thread. Another type of this lace is composed of the cambric motifs joined by "brides" where no net ground is used and is called Carrickmacross Guipure.

In bringing this little book to a close, I am fully aware that there are countless laces left unmentioned, and I

Illustration No. 73
Limerick. Needle-run lace; 19th century

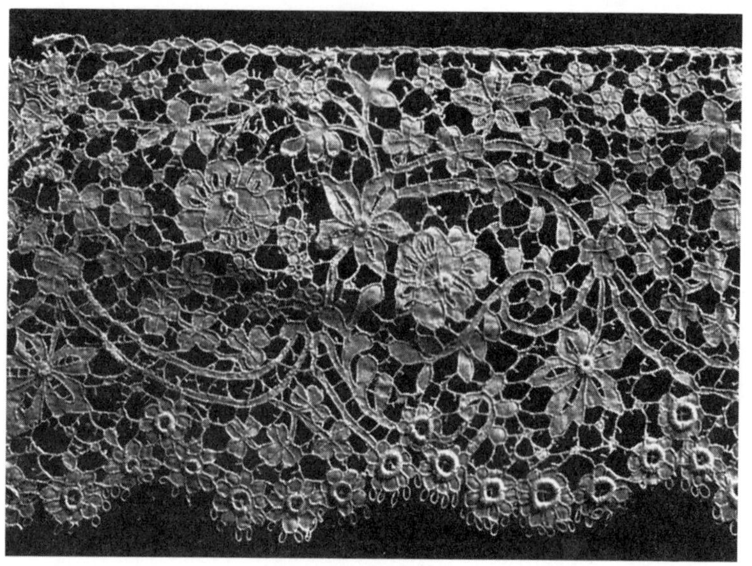

Illustration No. 74
Carrickmacross Guipure. Nineteenth century; showing cambric flowers cut out and stitched around

mean no slight to their beauty or interest, but they are not of sufficient prominence to be mentioned here, for they are little known outside of the locality in which they are made, save by collectors or students of lace.

We have passed lightly through three centuries of lace, which have produced exquisite examples of handiwork that can never be made again. For although lace-making is not a lost art, the marvelous creations that have been handed down to us will not, save in rare instances, be reproduced.

The hurried life of modern man, or rather modern woman, leaves little or no time for the patient clicking of bobbins or plying of needles for months and even years in the execution of a single masterpiece. While the scientific progress of the age has brought us many wonders, the machine has robbed the artistic world of the objects that only the patience and skill of the hand can accomplish. Real lace will continue to be made in ever increasing quantities and of undoubted merit, but the marvels demanded by kings and queens will not be repeated. For the same religious fervor that inspired man to build his glorious cathedrals, and woman to lavish the perfection of her handiwork on the vestments of the church, has passed with the centuries that have left us these memories.

"The love of beauty is taste—the creation of beauty is art."

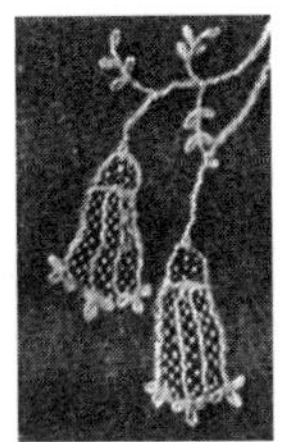

Glossary

Brides	Bars, connecting links.
Cote	Thread edge on Angleterre motifs.
Cordonnet	Raised outline.
Foliated	Leaf design.
Fond	Ground or mesh.
Fontanges	Head-dress. Period of Louis XIV.
Hexagonal	Six-sided.
Motifs	Separate designs.
Picot	Looped thread.
Punto Tirato . . .	Drawn-work.
Punto Tagliato . .	Cut-work.
Réseau	Ground or mesh.
Relief	Raised part of design.
Toilé	Solid part of lace.

Grounds

Fond Chant . . .	Six-pointed star—Point de Paris.
Fond Clair . . .	Light plain mesh—Lille.
Fond Simple . . .	Light plain mesh—Lille.
Fond à la Vierge .	Heavy five-hole—Binche.
Fond Cinq Trous .	Heavy five-hole—Binche.
Fond de Neige . .	Dotted disc ground—Binche and Val.
Fond Œil de Perdrix	Dotted disc ground—Binche and Val.
Hexagonal twisted .	Six-sided needle mesh—Alençon.
Hexagonal buttonholed	Six-sided needle mesh—Argentan.
Hexagonal plaited .	Bobbin mesh—Malines.
Hexagonal plaited .	Lozenge-shaped bobbin mesh—Angleterre
Réseau-Rosacé . .	Diapered ground.

INDEX

A CATALOG OF SELECTED

DOVER BOOKS

IN ALL FIELDS OF INTEREST

A CATALOG OF SELECTED DOVER BOOKS IN ALL FIELDS OF INTEREST

CONCERNING THE SPIRITUAL IN ART, Wassily Kandinsky. Pioneering work by father of abstract art. Thoughts on color theory, nature of art. Analysis of earlier masters. 12 illustrations. 80pp. of text. 5⅜ x 8½. 23411-8

ANIMALS: 1,419 Copyright-Free Illustrations of Mammals, Birds, Fish, Insects, etc., Jim Harter (ed.). Clear wood engravings present, in extremely lifelike poses, over 1,000 species of animals. One of the most extensive pictorial sourcebooks of its kind. Captions. Index. 284pp. 9 x 12. 23766-4

CELTIC ART: The Methods of Construction, George Bain. Simple geometric techniques for making Celtic interlacements, spirals, Kells-type initials, animals, humans, etc. Over 500 illustrations. 160pp. 9 x 12. (Available in U.S. only.) 22923-8

AN ATLAS OF ANATOMY FOR ARTISTS, Fritz Schider. Most thorough reference work on art anatomy in the world. Hundreds of illustrations, including selections from works by Vesalius, Leonardo, Goya, Ingres, Michelangelo, others. 593 illustrations. 192pp. 7⅛ x 10¼. 20241-0

CELTIC HAND STROKE-BY-STROKE (Irish Half-Uncial from "The Book of Kells"): An Arthur Baker Calligraphy Manual, Arthur Baker. Complete guide to creating each letter of the alphabet in distinctive Celtic manner. Covers hand position, strokes, pens, inks, paper, more. Illustrated. 48pp. 8¼ x 11. 24336-2

EASY ORIGAMI, John Montroll. Charming collection of 32 projects (hat, cup, pelican, piano, swan, many more) specially designed for the novice origami hobbyist. Clearly illustrated easy-to-follow instructions insure that even beginning papercrafters will achieve successful results. 48pp. 8¼ x 11. 27298-2

THE COMPLETE BOOK OF BIRDHOUSE CONSTRUCTION FOR WOODWORKERS, Scott D. Campbell. Detailed instructions, illustrations, tables. Also data on bird habitat and instinct patterns. Bibliography. 3 tables. 63 illustrations in 15 figures. 48pp. 5¼ x 8½. 24407-5

BLOOMINGDALE'S ILLUSTRATED 1886 CATALOG: Fashions, Dry Goods and Housewares, Bloomingdale Brothers. Famed merchants' extremely rare catalog depicting about 1,700 products: clothing, housewares, firearms, dry goods, jewelry, more. Invaluable for dating, identifying vintage items. Also, copyright-free graphics for artists, designers. Co-published with Henry Ford Museum & Greenfield Village. 160pp. 8¼ x 11. 25780-0

HISTORIC COSTUME IN PICTURES, Braun & Schneider. Over 1,450 costumed figures in clearly detailed engravings–from dawn of civilization to end of 19th century. Captions. Many folk costumes. 256pp. 8⅜ x 11¾. 23150-X

THE BEST TALES OF HOFFMANN, E. T. A. Hoffmann. 10 of Hoffmann's most important stories: "Nutcracker and the King of Mice," "The Golden Flowerpot," etc. 458pp. 5⅜ x 8½. 21793-0

FROM FETISH TO GOD IN ANCIENT EGYPT, E. A. Wallis Budge. Rich detailed survey of Egyptian conception of "God" and gods, magic, cult of animals, Osiris, more. Also, superb English translations of hymns and legends. 240 illustrations. 545pp. 5⅜ x 8½. 25803-3

FRENCH STORIES/CONTES FRANÇAIS: A Dual-Language Book, Wallace Fowlie. Ten stories by French masters, Voltaire to Camus: "Micromegas" by Voltaire; "The Atheist's Mass" by Balzac; "Minuet" by de Maupassant; "The Guest" by Camus, six more. Excellent English translations on facing pages. Also French-English vocabulary list, exercises, more. 352pp. 5⅜ x 8½. 26443-2

CHICAGO AT THE TURN OF THE CENTURY IN PHOTOGRAPHS: 122 Historic Views from the Collections of the Chicago Historical Society, Larry A. Viskochil. Rare large-format prints offer detailed views of City Hall, State Street, the Loop, Hull House, Union Station, many other landmarks, circa 1904-1913. Introduction. Captions. Maps. 144pp. 9⅜ x 12¼. 24656-6

OLD BROOKLYN IN EARLY PHOTOGRAPHS, 1865-1929, William Lee Younger. Luna Park, Gravesend race track, construction of Grand Army Plaza, moving of Hotel Brighton, etc. 157 previously unpublished photographs. 165pp. 8⅞ x 11¾. 23587-4

THE MYTHS OF THE NORTH AMERICAN INDIANS, Lewis Spence. Rich anthology of the myths and legends of the Algonquins, Iroquois, Pawnees and Sioux, prefaced by an extensive historical and ethnological commentary. 36 illustrations. 480pp. 5⅜ x 8½. 25967-6

AN ENCYCLOPEDIA OF BATTLES: Accounts of Over 1,560 Battles from 1479 B.C. to the Present, David Eggenberger. Essential details of every major battle in recorded history from the first battle of Megiddo in 1479 B.C. to Grenada in 1984. List of Battle Maps. New Appendix covering the years 1967-1984. Index. 99 illustrations. 544pp. 6½ x 9¼. 24913-1

SAILING ALONE AROUND THE WORLD, Captain Joshua Slocum. First man to sail around the world, alone, in small boat. One of great feats of seamanship told in delightful manner. 67 illustrations. 294pp. 5⅜ x 8½. 20326-3

ANARCHISM AND OTHER ESSAYS, Emma Goldman. Powerful, penetrating, prophetic essays on direct action, role of minorities, prison reform, puritan hypocrisy, violence, etc. 271pp. 5⅜ x 8½. 22484-8

MYTHS OF THE HINDUS AND BUDDHISTS, Ananda K. Coomaraswamy and Sister Nivedita. Great stories of the epics; deeds of Krishna, Shiva, taken from puranas, Vedas, folk tales; etc. 32 illustrations. 400pp. 5⅜ x 8½. 21759-0

THE TRAUMA OF BIRTH, Otto Rank. Rank's controversial thesis that anxiety neurosis is caused by profound psychological trauma which occurs at birth. 256pp. 5⅜ x 8½. 27974-X

A THEOLOGICO-POLITICAL TREATISE, Benedict Spinoza. Also contains unfinished Political Treatise. Great classic on religious liberty, theory of government on common consent. R. Elwes translation. Total of 421pp. 5⅜ x 8½. 20249-6

MY BONDAGE AND MY FREEDOM, Frederick Douglass. Born a slave, Douglass became outspoken force in antislavery movement. The best of Douglass' autobiographies. Graphic description of slave life. 464pp. 5⅜ x 8½. 22457-0

FOLLOWING THE EQUATOR: A Journey Around the World, Mark Twain. Fascinating humorous account of 1897 voyage to Hawaii, Australia, India, New Zealand, etc. Ironic, bemused reports on peoples, customs, climate, flora and fauna, politics, much more. 197 illustrations. 720pp. 5⅜ x 8½. 26113-1

THE PEOPLE CALLED SHAKERS, Edward D. Andrews. Definitive study of Shakers: origins, beliefs, practices, dances, social organization, furniture and crafts, etc. 33 illustrations. 351pp. 5⅜ x 8½. 21081-2

THE MYTHS OF GREECE AND ROME, H. A. Guerber. A classic of mythology, generously illustrated, long prized for its simple, graphic, accurate retelling of the principal myths of Greece and Rome, and for its commentary on their origins and significance. With 64 illustrations by Michelangelo, Raphael, Titian, Rubens, Canova, Bernini and others. 480pp. 5⅜ x 8½. 27584-1

PSYCHOLOGY OF MUSIC, Carl E. Seashore. Classic work discusses music as a medium from psychological viewpoint. Clear treatment of physical acoustics, auditory apparatus, sound perception, development of musical skills, nature of musical feeling, host of other topics. 88 figures. 408pp. 5⅜ x 8½. 21851-1

THE PHILOSOPHY OF HISTORY, Georg W. Hegel. Great classic of Western thought develops concept that history is not chance but rational process, the evolution of freedom. 457pp. 5⅜ x 8½. 20112-0

THE BOOK OF TEA, Kakuzo Okakura. Minor classic of the Orient: entertaining, charming explanation, interpretation of traditional Japanese culture in terms of tea ceremony. 94pp. 5⅜ x 8½. 20070-1

LIFE IN ANCIENT EGYPT, Adolf Erman. Fullest, most thorough, detailed older account with much not in more recent books, domestic life, religion, magic, medicine, commerce, much more. Many illustrations reproduce tomb paintings, carvings, hieroglyphs, etc. 597pp. 5⅜ x 8½. 22632-8

SUNDIALS, Their Theory and Construction, Albert Waugh. Far and away the best, most thorough coverage of ideas, mathematics concerned, types, construction, adjusting anywhere. Simple, nontechnical treatment allows even children to build several of these dials. Over 100 illustrations. 230pp. 5⅜ x 8½. 22947-5

THEORETICAL HYDRODYNAMICS, L. M. Milne-Thomson. Classic exposition of the mathematical theory of fluid motion, applicable to both hydrodynamics and aerodynamics. Over 600 exercises. 768pp. 6⅛ x 9¼. 68970-0

SONGS OF EXPERIENCE: Facsimile Reproduction with 26 Plates in Full Color, William Blake. 26 full-color plates from a rare 1826 edition. Includes "The Tyger," "London," "Holy Thursday," and other poems. Printed text of poems. 48pp. 5¼ x 7. 24636-1

OLD-TIME VIGNETTES IN FULL COLOR, Carol Belanger Grafton (ed.). Over 390 charming, often sentimental illustrations, selected from archives of Victorian graphics–pretty women posing, children playing, food, flowers, kittens and puppies, smiling cherubs, birds and butterflies, much more. All copyright-free. 48pp. 9¼ x 12¼. 27269-9

LITTLE BOOK OF EARLY AMERICAN CRAFTS AND TRADES, Peter Stockham (ed.). 1807 children's book explains crafts and trades: baker, hatter, cooper, potter, and many others. 23 copperplate illustrations. 140pp. 4⅝ x 6. 23336-7

VICTORIAN FASHIONS AND COSTUMES FROM HARPER'S BAZAR, 1867–1898, Stella Blum (ed.). Day costumes, evening wear, sports clothes, shoes, hats, other accessories in over 1,000 detailed engravings. 320pp. 9⅜ x 12¼. 22990-4

GUSTAV STICKLEY, THE CRAFTSMAN, Mary Ann Smith. Superb study surveys broad scope of Stickley's achievement, especially in architecture. Design philosophy, rise and fall of the Craftsman empire, descriptions and floor plans for many Craftsman houses, more. 86 black-and-white halftones. 31 line illustrations. Introduction 208pp. 6½ x 9¼. 27210-9

THE LONG ISLAND RAIL ROAD IN EARLY PHOTOGRAPHS, Ron Ziel. Over 220 rare photos, informative text document origin (1844) and development of rail service on Long Island. Vintage views of early trains, locomotives, stations, passengers, crews, much more. Captions. 8⅞ x 11¾. 26301-0

VOYAGE OF THE LIBERDADE, Joshua Slocum. Great 19th-century mariner's thrilling, first-hand account of the wreck of his ship off South America, the 35-foot boat he built from the wreckage, and its remarkable voyage home. 128pp. 5⅜ x 8½. 40022-0

TEN BOOKS ON ARCHITECTURE, Vitruvius. The most important book ever written on architecture. Early Roman aesthetics, technology, classical orders, site selection, all other aspects. Morgan translation. 331pp. 5⅜ x 8½. 20645-9

THE HUMAN FIGURE IN MOTION, Eadweard Muybridge. More than 4,500 stopped-action photos, in action series, showing undraped men, women, children jumping, lying down, throwing, sitting, wrestling, carrying, etc. 390pp. 7⅞ x 10⅝. 20204-6 Clothbd.

TREES OF THE EASTERN AND CENTRAL UNITED STATES AND CANADA, William M. Harlow. Best one-volume guide to 140 trees. Full descriptions, woodlore, range, etc. Over 600 illustrations. Handy size. 288pp. 4½ x 6⅜. 20395-6

SONGS OF WESTERN BIRDS, Dr. Donald J. Borror. Complete song and call repertoire of 60 western species, including flycatchers, juncoes, cactus wrens, many more–includes fully illustrated booklet. Cassette and manual 99913-0

GROWING AND USING HERBS AND SPICES, Milo Miloradovich. Versatile handbook provides all the information needed for cultivation and use of all the herbs and spices available in North America. 4 illustrations. Index. Glossary. 236pp. 5⅜ x 8½. 25058-X

BIG BOOK OF MAZES AND LABYRINTHS, Walter Shepherd. 50 mazes and labyrinths in all–classical, solid, ripple, and more–in one great volume. Perfect inexpensive puzzler for clever youngsters. Full solutions. 112pp. 8⅛ x 11. 22951-3

THE WIT AND HUMOR OF OSCAR WILDE, Alvin Redman (ed.). More than 1,000 ripostes, paradoxes, wisecracks: Work is the curse of the drinking classes; I can resist everything except temptation; etc. 258pp. 5⅜ x 8½. 20602-5

SHAKESPEARE LEXICON AND QUOTATION DICTIONARY, Alexander Schmidt. Full definitions, locations, shades of meaning in every word in plays and poems. More than 50,000 exact quotations. 1,485pp. 6½ x 9¼. 2-vol. set.
Vol. 1: 22726-X
Vol. 2: 22727-8

SELECTED POEMS, Emily Dickinson. Over 100 best-known, best-loved poems by one of America's foremost poets, reprinted from authoritative early editions. No comparable edition at this price. Index of first lines. 64pp. 5³⁄₁₆ x 8¼. 26466-1

THE INSIDIOUS DR. FU-MANCHU, Sax Rohmer. The first of the popular mystery series introduces a pair of English detectives to their archnemesis, the diabolical Dr. Fu-Manchu. Flavorful atmosphere, fast-paced action, and colorful characters enliven this classic of the genre. 208pp. 5³⁄₁₆ x 8¼. 29898-1

THE MALLEUS MALEFICARUM OF KRAMER AND SPRENGER, translated by Montague Summers. Full text of most important witchhunter's "bible," used by both Catholics and Protestants. 278pp. 6⅝ x 10. 22802-9

SPANISH STORIES/CUENTOS ESPAÑOLES: A Dual-Language Book, Angel Flores (ed.). Unique format offers 13 great stories in Spanish by Cervantes, Borges, others. Faithful English translations on facing pages. 352pp. 5⅜ x 8½. 25399-6

GARDEN CITY, LONG ISLAND, IN EARLY PHOTOGRAPHS, 1869–1919, Mildred H. Smith. Handsome treasury of 118 vintage pictures, accompanied by carefully researched captions, document the Garden City Hotel fire (1899), the Vanderbilt Cup Race (1908), the first airmail flight departing from the Nassau Boulevard Aerodrome (1911), and much more. 96pp. 8⅞ x 11¾. 40669-5

OLD QUEENS, N.Y., IN EARLY PHOTOGRAPHS, Vincent F. Seyfried and William Asadorian. Over 160 rare photographs of Maspeth, Jamaica, Jackson Heights, and other areas. Vintage views of DeWitt Clinton mansion, 1939 World's Fair and more. Captions. 192pp. 8⅞ x 11. 26358-4

CAPTURED BY THE INDIANS: 15 Firsthand Accounts, 1750-1870, Frederick Drimmer. Astounding true historical accounts of grisly torture, bloody conflicts, relentless pursuits, miraculous escapes and more, by people who lived to tell the tale. 384pp. 5⅜ x 8½. 24901-8

THE WORLD'S GREAT SPEECHES (Fourth Enlarged Edition), Lewis Copeland, Lawrence W. Lamm, and Stephen J. McKenna. Nearly 300 speeches provide public speakers with a wealth of updated quotes and inspiration–from Pericles' funeral oration and William Jennings Bryan's "Cross of Gold Speech" to Malcolm X's powerful words on the Black Revolution and Earl of Spenser's tribute to his sister, Diana, Princess of Wales. 944pp. 5⅜ x 8⅜. 40903-1

THE BOOK OF THE SWORD, Sir Richard F. Burton. Great Victorian scholar/adventurer's eloquent, erudite history of the "queen of weapons"–from prehistory to early Roman Empire. Evolution and development of early swords, variations (sabre, broadsword, cutlass, scimitar, etc.), much more. 336pp. 6⅛ x 9¼. 25434-8

CATALOG OF DOVER BOOKS

THE STORY OF THE TITANIC AS TOLD BY ITS SURVIVORS, Jack Winocour (ed.). What it was really like. Panic, despair, shocking inefficiency, and a little heroism. More thrilling than any fictional account. 26 illustrations. 320pp. 5⅜ x 8½. 20610-6

FAIRY AND FOLK TALES OF THE IRISH PEASANTRY, William Butler Yeats (ed.). Treasury of 64 tales from the twilight world of Celtic myth and legend: "The Soul Cages," "The Kildare Pooka," "King O'Toole and his Goose," many more. Introduction and Notes by W. B. Yeats. 352pp. 5⅜ x 8½. 26941-8

BUDDHIST MAHAYANA TEXTS, E. B. Cowell and others (eds.). Superb, accurate translations of basic documents in Mahayana Buddhism, highly important in history of religions. The Buddha-karita of Asvaghosha, Larger Sukhavativyuha, more. 448pp. 5⅜ x 8½. 25552-2

ONE TWO THREE . . . INFINITY: Facts and Speculations of Science, George Gamow. Great physicist's fascinating, readable overview of contemporary science: number theory, relativity, fourth dimension, entropy, genes, atomic structure, much more. 128 illustrations. Index. 352pp. 5⅜ x 8½. 25664-2

EXPERIMENTATION AND MEASUREMENT, W. J. Youden. Introductory manual explains laws of measurement in simple terms and offers tips for achieving accuracy and minimizing errors. Mathematics of measurement, use of instruments, experimenting with machines. 1994 edition. Foreword. Preface. Introduction. Epilogue. Selected Readings. Glossary. Index. Tables and figures. 128pp. 5⅜ x 8½. 40451-X

DALÍ ON MODERN ART: The Cuckolds of Antiquated Modern Art, Salvador Dalí. Influential painter skewers modern art and its practitioners. Outrageous evaluations of Picasso, Cézanne, Turner, more. 15 renderings of paintings discussed. 44 calligraphic decorations by Dalí. 96pp. 5⅜ x 8½. (Available in U.S. only.) 29220-7

ANTIQUE PLAYING CARDS: A Pictorial History, Henry René D'Allemagne. Over 900 elaborate, decorative images from rare playing cards (14th–20th centuries): Bacchus, death, dancing dogs, hunting scenes, royal coats of arms, players cheating, much more. 96pp. 9¼ x 12¼. 29265-7

MAKING FURNITURE MASTERPIECES: 30 Projects with Measured Drawings, Franklin H. Gottshall. Step-by-step instructions, illustrations for constructing handsome, useful pieces, among them a Sheraton desk, Chippendale chair, Spanish desk, Queen Anne table and a William and Mary dressing mirror. 224pp. 8⅛ x 11¼. 29338-6

THE FOSSIL BOOK: A Record of Prehistoric Life, Patricia V. Rich et al. Profusely illustrated definitive guide covers everything from single-celled organisms and dinosaurs to birds and mammals and the interplay between climate and man. Over 1,500 illustrations. 760pp. 7½ x 10⅛. 29371-8

Paperbound unless otherwise indicated. Available at your book dealer, online at **www.doverpublications.com**, or by writing to Dept. GI, Dover Publications, Inc., 31 East 2nd Street, Mineola, NY 11501. For current price information or for free catalogues (please indicate field of interest), write to Dover Publications or log on to **www.doverpublications.com** and see every Dover book in print. Dover publishes more than 500 books each year on science, elementary and advanced mathematics, biology, music, art, literary history, social sciences, and other areas.